GOOD THINGS THAT HAPPEN AS YOU GROW OLDER

Lauraine Snelling

BRISTOL PUBLISHING ENTERPRISES
San Leandro, California

Printed in the United States of America.

ISBN 1-55867-036-X

Library of Congress Catalog Card Number: 92-70505

Cover design: Frank Paredes

To my mother,
a dynamite example of active aging
who also loves unconditionally.

And to all those who shared
their thoughts, feelings and experiences
with me — thank you. You are incredible!

PREFACE

Old age used to come early in life, and it was usually brief. Everyone dreaded it, because it was always seen as a series of losses: youth, beauty, jobs, loved ones, health, brain power, time, abilities of all kinds. But now we know new truths about how the body ages and plenty of good things about growing older!

I went to the people who really know, people 50 years old and beyond, and asked the question, "What good things are happening to you as you grow older?" What an incredible font of energy, enthusiasm, wisdom and pure fun I tapped. I asked famous people and ordinary people, hundreds of people. I asked for reactions from audiences to whom I spoke. I asked the question to groups of which I was a member. I read books written on the subject. I observed interviews on television. I reviewed magazines.

This book is the result of that effort. Many, many people mentioned the same things. (Everyone didn't agree that all of these good things happened to them, and you probably won't, either.) I have included only some of the responses — those most representative, or most interesting, or funniest. Sometimes I knew the name of the person who spoke, sometimes I did not, and sometimes the person preferred not to be identified.

Since I am an incurable optimist, writing this book helped me compile and catalogue my feelings on growing older as well. I have to admit that like you, I've had doubts about getting older. But then I figured it out. What are your choices? Grow old or die – grow old living a rich, satisfying life or one of sedentary misery. No matter how you approach life, you'll still be 50 or 70 or 90. You make the choice to sigh or celebrate.

> *Grow old along with me!*
> *The best is yet to be . . .*
> Robert Browning

The focus of this book is on growth, wisdom, fun and freedom, and I hope these voices will inspire you as they have me.

Lauraine Snelling
Martinez, California

YOUR ATTITUDES CHANGE

"My attitudes have changed most definitely, everything from the way I see the world to the way I read people. I hope I've become more forgiving, less judgmental, more willing to live and let live. I'm working on accepting people as they are, right this moment. I'm trying to allow myself the same privilege, accepting the fact that everything we hear, see, feel changes for everyone of us, every moment of our life, making each of us a kaleidoscope. The more colorful we are the more exciting life is."

Gail Grundon, who sees growth and change as necessary ingredients for an exciting life.

"When I was younger, I thought people were old at 60 and now that I'm in my 50s, I think old is 80s and above. But to be truly honest, I realize that age and old aren't the same. Age is chronological years and old is a state of mind. I think my attitudes to other things changed, too. I wonder more, meaning I look at this world and all that's in it through a state of awe. Time, people and I are more precious. I appreciate life and living more than I ever did before."

Barbara Branson, who finds excitement in life.

"The inner attitude of your mind dictates the outer aspects of your life."

*Art Linkletter, host of **Houseparty**, author, preacher of positive aging.*

"Your attitude toward aging is very important in retirement. You must know that you can grow older without being old, that your chronological age need not conform to biological age. You must remember, too, that on any day, including anniversaries, you are only a day older than the day before—and also, that each day is the first day of the rest of your life"

*Harry Disston, from his book **Wear Out, Don't Rust Out!***

2

YOU BECOME MORE REALISTIC

"After 50 or 55, there's a new kind of idealism. It's mellower than the idealism of youth, that succumbed to money and things and getting ahead. You start thinking more about what's really going on. I deeply believe a line I came up with at a meeting on the state of the state of Oregon. 'While nothing stays the same, some things never change.' It fits."
Weatherman Jim Bosley, from Channel 2 in Portland, Oregon.

"When you're young you think that everything should be perfect, and if it weren't for wrong-thinking people, it would be. No one should be poor, there should be no war, nor hungry, nor homeless, nor disease, nor crime, nor pollution — and of course, we do want these terrible things to end. But as you grow older, you realize more clearly what it takes to make things happen, and even though you may work for these causes and others, your view is more realistic. How many people I meet in my age group who say that their position has changed from their idealistic youth!"
P.B., observer.

"Now I'm entering a new phase with a new gift — the gift of experience. I have my past, all that's come before, to learn from. With this I can rechart a course for the time that remains, based not on myth and romance but rather on reality and self-knowledge. There must be no 'if only's' about the things that really matter —"

*Jane Fonda, from **Women Coming of Age**.*

3 YOU LEARN TO COPE WITH STRESS

"Procrastination is the number one cause of tension. It causes more heart attacks and strokes than anything else. You always worry about the things you put off. . . . so, I'm a great believer in getting things taken care of fast. And then I reward myself with a little leisure. That way I don't lose energy worrying."
*Wise advice from Bob Hope in **The Saturday Evening Post**, October 1981.*

"[As we get older] we are in search of serenity. Overload is out, tranquility is in; that is a necessary requirement for growing older gracefully."
*Eda LeShan, from **It's Better To Be Over The Hill Than Under It.***

"The most recent information supports your insurance company's claim that health usually improves after retirement. If you're forced to retire because of health, retirement isn't necessarily going to make you better. But if retirement brings a release from stress and pressures, chances are you may feel years younger in just a few weeks."
*Leo Hauser and Vincent A. Miller, in **Retirement.***

5

4 YOU BECOME MORE MELLOW

"I believe you become more mellow with age. You've learned not to let things bother you so much. All the knocks and bruises you've gotten through life now grant you the gift of mellow wisdom."

Dr. Effie Chow, founder of The East/West Academy of Healing Arts.

"I'm much more relaxed and laid back and while I've always had a good sense of humor, now I enjoy laughter even more. I still have a tendency to overreact but I can see the humor in things more easily."

Marlys Gilbert, who's having a ball in a new career.

"I guess I take things a little easier. If things don't go the way you want, well, I just don't take it so seriously. I've always had a good sense of humor and I think it's gotten better. 'Course a lot of people think I'm nuts."

Bob Rheinhart, who's believed in laughing all his life.

"I feel at peace and I don't like chaos, although sometimes I create chaos."

*Elizabeth Taylor, turning 60, in **Good House-keeping**, February, 1992.*

"You're not tied to perfection so much as you grow older. You know, you go with the flow, more relaxed. It used to be if you had guests, why, dear, dear, everything had to be just perfect. Now, well, if the dinner isn't quite done on time, who cares?"

Carolyn Bolles, owner of a bed and breakfast inn.

5 YOU BECOME MORE TOLERANT

"I believe I've become much more tolerant as I've aged. I'm more willing to put up with other people's crazinesses. Maybe it's because I've learned to think more of myself. I really don't care what others think anymore. I'm my own person and I like that."

Dotty Bingham, living life to the fullest.

"We have an interracial marriage right in our tight group and for a boy from the deep South and with my upbringing all those years ago, that would have been unbelievable. Now I just sort of notice and accept people for who they are. I don't care what color or sex they are, if they're nice people and are trying to be helpful, team players, then I'm all for them."

Phil Oestricher, a southern boy with retired attitudes.

"You become more tolerant and loving of those important people around you, especially old friends, who are gold, and your family. You overlook people who lie to you, or don't show up or whatever because you realize that's the way of

8

humankind. That's the way it is. It's an uneven playing field. But go for it anyway."
Art Linkletter, TV personality, author, philosopher.

"As you understand your own weaknesses, you become much more tolerant of others."
John George, who is trying to overcome perfectionism.

"The biggest problem we've got is that we're all so bloomin' human."
L.S., armchair philosopher and another recovering perfectionist.

"I've learned in my years that when people are short-tempered or bossy, ungenerous or thoughtless, that's just the way they are. It has nothing to do with me. If the light turns green at the same time as the person behind you honks the horn, that just means he's an impatient person. You don't have to go around feeling bad all day."
*Patricia Evans, author of **The Verbally Abusive Relationship.***

6 YOU BECOME MORE GRATEFUL

"I am happy. I have a happy nature — I like the rain — I like the sun — the heat — the cold — the mountains — the sea — the flowers — the — Well, I like life and I've been so lucky. Why shouldn't I be happy?"
*Katherine Hepburn, from her book **Me**.*

"You need an attitude of gratitude. Life is a half full glass and you need to be grateful for that. It's healthy physically and spiritually."
Dr. Herbert Schwartz, pediatric oncologist.

"I'll be grateful for every day I had in the President's house. And I'll thank God for it. Yes, I'll miss this. It's an extraordinary life. But there's still my husband, my grandchildren, and children and friends and Millie and our memories. I'll go on with this blessed life, happily digging away in my garden."
*First Lady Barbara Bush, in **Ladies Home Journal**, November 1990.*

YOU BECOME MORE UNDERSTANDING

"Maybe it's not until you get older that you get less concerned with yourself and can understand the reality of other people. Still, I don't get the same lift out of the young anymore that I now get out of the older people whom I've known for a long time."

Helen Hays, First Lady of American Theater, from an article in Redbook.

"I think understanding goes two ways, out towards other people and for yourself. As you get older and wiser, you can't really have one without the other. When I look back, reflect on who I am, I understand and accept others. As an editor I trained so many bright and enthusiastic journalists right out of college. It was easy to understand them because I had been there. Now I try to help widows around me get out and get going. I haven't been there yet, but I know since my husband is fighting cancer, I may be. And understanding them helps me look ahead."

Phyllis Roth, retired editor who is still being bitten by the writing bug.

ul. "The longer I live, the more understanding I become. At 40 I wasn't half as tolerant and understanding of what others were going through. But life hands us various challenges and mine came later. Now I can understand, accept and feel the various changes that have come into my life and those of my family and friends with compassion and warmth."

Rosalyne Marsh, who says each decade in life brings new wisdom and understanding.

YOU BECOME MORE CONTENT

Dot Latting has this poem hung where she can read it last thing at night and first thing in the morning. She says it helps keep her focused on the really important things and content with her life.

> You are as young as your faith,
> As young as your confidence,
> As young as your hopes.
> In the central place of every heart
> There is a recording chamber.
> So long as it receives messages
> Of beauty, hope, cheer and courage,
> So long are we young.
>
> *General Douglas MacArthur,*
> *thanks to Dot Latting.*

"Reality is important to me and I've learned to live for today. I travel. I enjoy myself. I spend time with my daughter. I love life. That's the way I hope to keep on going. I enjoy whatever it is I do. If I don't enjoy something, I don't do it."
*Cary Grant, in **Redbook**, March, 1987.*

"Enough is enough. I find this in all areas of my life. I know if I wanted, I could go out and buy

something I'd like but I have what I need, most of what I want and — enough is enough."
Jade Snow Wong, writer, artist, business owner.

"I'm more comfortable with myself now. All my life I measured myself against others and always came up short. I was overly concerned over how 'they' were going to view me or think of me. So it would keep me from doing something I wanted because I might fail, get egg on my face. That doesn't matter any more. I know part of this contentment comes from my relationship with God, my relationships with others of strong faith. I'm more open, willing to share, since I'm more comfortable with myself. It's okay to say what I'm feeling."
Pat Cavnar, who feels she's coming of age.

"After 50 you become more content. Especially when your children are out of college and married. It's like you start a whole new life. We call it the second honeymoon — you can sit back and enjoy each other."
Irene McWhorter, who's only 62 and loving the lifestyle she and her husband worked hard for.

YOU REALIZE YOUR PERSONAL POWER

"One of the great changes that being over 50 brings is the ability to have more power over your life. All the strengths you accumulate during a lifetime are there to serve you and carry you through any crisis. No one incident becomes a tragedy that can't be handled through the faith, wisdom and knowledge you've developed. The older you get, the stronger you grow. Call it 'personal power' — the ability to use your brain to control your life in ways that youth doesn't know exist — to be in control of your life instead of letting other people, social trends, circumstances and more dictate what or who you'll become. Personal power gives you energy and license to be yourself. Would I trade my 61 years to be in my early 20s? Never!"

Ruby MacDonald, who constantly explores new ways to become all that she can be.

"My inner strength has always come from family, faith and friends."

*First Lady Barbara Bush, from **Ladies Home Journal**, November 1990.*

"Problems are good for you because then you have to solve them. Every problem has a solution if you persist and discover it."

Norman Vincent Peale, master of communicating complicated truths in simple language.

"With maturity often comes understanding that you *can* solve problems, that every problem has a solution, which ends feelings of frustration and defeat. My mother taught me, '*Can't* never did anything! *Can* did it all!' She was a wise woman, and helped to create a capable daughter. "

P.B., still solving problems.

10   YOU BECOME MORE JOYFUL

"Three things I've found in my old age. Wisdom, which I'm going to write a book about. I've always been smart, now I'm wise. Joy, because I'm happy whether it's happy around me or not. I seem to be happy all the time. No matter what awful things happen, there's some joyful part of me that cannot be moved, through traumas and everything. I began noticing this early in my 50s. The third is mercy. I no longer feel any judgment from God and maybe that's why I've become more and more merciful, more tolerant, more gentle."

Kristen Johnson Ingram, author.

"I'm 87 years old and I'm happier than I've ever been in my life. I enjoy every minute of it. Part of that is because I've always had a fulfilling career both as a pastor and a psychologist. But you know that old saying, so soon we get old, so late we get smart. With the years I feel an accumulation of wisdom and I believe I've learned more the last five years than ever. I write, travel and all the time, I learn from people. If you love people, you get it all back."

Dr. Cecil Osborne, who helps to change lives.

11 YOU DEVELOP A BETTER SENSE OF HUMOR

"I think one of the things I inherited from my father was a good sense of humor. How do you get through life without one? But now the things that amuse me greatly are the funny little things, like the antics of the cat, word plays, my grandchildren."
Jen Southworth, who needed a good sense of humor in her years of teaching high school.

"You have to go through life with a wry sense of humor. You have to realize that apart from the military or the police, no decision is irrevocable or irreparable. People spend too much time worrying about their decisions. When you can bring some laughter to a situation or at least not take things too seriously, least of all yourself, you'll be welcome everywhere."
Tony Barrett, who laughes even more these days.

"The never-fail rule for feeling better about being older is maintaining a sense of humor. One charming grande dame in Colorado claims she copes with her failing memory by feeling her toothbrush before she brushes her teeth. If it's wet, of course, she knows she's already done that. What a young outlook she has! and what a joy she is to be around."

*Frances Weaver, in **The Girls with the Grandmother Faces.***

"Sixty is a great age to be," said Elizabeth Taylor. "At my age a woman can make anything out of life she wants. You can lay back and become elderly or you can hitch up your jeans and go forward because you have experience and expertise you didn't have before . . . . You can do things that are completely off the wall and get away with it. Stuff you never could have pulled off when you were younger. You can have a ball with life if you want. Or you can become a couch potato and let life slide right by.

"By 60, you should have a terrific sense of humor, especially about yourself. You'd probably want to commit suicide at my age without humor. I look around me and I'm amazed at all the things, good and bad, that have happened in my lifetime. My mother is 95 and it's even more amazing to her."

*Elizabeth Taylor in **Good Housekeeping**, February 1992.*

"A sense of humor is your most important resource. It is the most valuable gift given to us by our Creator, and the highest form of wisdom."

*Ann and Robert Redd, in their book, **Whimsey, Wit and Wisdom.***

12 YOU CAN LAUGH AT YOURSELF

George Burns is talking. "It's ten in the morning, Sarah's in bed, and she says to her husband, 'Sam, be a good boy, go to the deli and bring me a hot pastrami on rye.'

'Hot pastrami on rye,' he repeats.

'With lots of mustard,' she says, 'and write it down, you shouldn't forget.'

'I won't forget. You want a hot pastrami on rye with lots of mustard.'

'And have them throw in a big kosher dill pickle.'

'Fine,' he says and starts to walk out. She says, 'Sam, you'll forget. Write it down!' He says, 'I don't have to write it down. You want a hot pastrami on rye with lots of mustard and a big kosher pickle.' And out he goes. Twenty minutes later he's back with a plate of salami and eggs.

'Sam,' she hollers, 'I told you to write it down.'

'Why, what's wrong?'

'You forgot the bagel!'

"Some people are reluctant to tell jokes like that. They're afraid it might be taken as lack of concern for the wear and tear old people have to put up with. From what I've seen, they can't be more wrong. Old people can't wait to tell these same jokes to each other. I don't know of any group less sensitive about themselves than the elderly, or more able to laugh at their shortcomings."

George Burns, who in his mid-90s wrote **Wisdom of the Nineties.**

"You have to learn to laugh at the changes in you as you age. My photographer friends moan about not being able to get down to do the shoots. But that's not the worst part, it's getting up again."

Ruth Heintz, who's learned to be creative to get to do what she wants, even at 70.

X

13 YOU BECOME MORE OPTIMISTIC

"The ups and downs, the problems and stress, along with all the happiness, have given me optimism and hope because I am living proof of survival. The things I've come through would have felled an ox."

Elizabeth Taylor on turning 60, from an article in **Good Housekeeping**, *February 1992.*

"A study by Stella Chess says that people are born optimistic or serious. When I try to fit myself into that profile, I look back and see pictures of a smiling child. I believe I had a happy childhood and I'm sure that contributes to my feelings of optimism. But as I've grown, I realize that we must *choose* to look on the good side of things. To be focused on the bad or down side is self-indulgence."

A woman who teaches and helps others.

"I believe in miracles. I believe that here we are and we can be in severe physical trouble. but if our spirits aren't in severe physical trouble, then we can rise up out of it. You've got to be able to dream."

Katherine Hepburn, from her book **Me**.

14 ⬥ YOU LEARN TO ACCEPT CHANGE

"I'm learning how vitally important it is to say good-bye. As things change in our lives we need to let go, say goodbye and move on through the new doors that are ever opening. People are especially reluctant to give up their pain and say goodbye to it. They hang onto it. It is almost better to have the pain than the unknown. But it's not healthy and stops growth."

Louise Lothspeich, counselor.

"I hear people say that old people don't adjust to change. Doesn't make sense to me. Look at all the change that's gone on since I was born. Automobiles hit the roads, we learned to fly, two world wars, the Great Depression (I didn't think it was so great but then I was just a kid), telephones, television, space travel, a man on the moon, the wall went up in Berlin and now the wall came down, I ran a business, had a wife and kids, bought a home, lost my wife a few years ago and now live in a retirement community. And you say I don't accept change?"

Jack Forde, who plays the meanest game of blackjack around.

YOU REALIZE YOU ARE ON A SPIRITUAL JOURNEY

"I believe I have come through the first three stages of spiritual growth that Scott Peck talked about in a workshop; one is the home, the first attempts to get an answer to the question 'why?' Two is the institution, church, nation and three is asking questions where it becomes uncomfortable, especially if you stay there. Four is the stage of universality, when you go beyond the questions and finite answers and develop a compassion for humanity. This is where unconditional love comes in. I'm not there yet, but the training and the kind of work I'm in makes that more possible.

"I believe the Holy Spirit is really moving in our times; I sense such an unfolding."

Louise Lochspeith, counselor.

"I *know* I am on a spiritual path, just the early part. In my last life it was 'kindergarten,' and now it's first grade. I'll graduate after this life to the next learning experience, and take what I have learned with me — that's why I don't fear death."

Alice Musgrove, 63, learning as she goes.

"I never had any religious education but I had an interior drive that has shown up at various times in my life. I wrote a poem in my teens called, *I Walk with God*, even though I had no relationship with a synagogue. Once, as a pediatrician, I had a child who was close to dying and I didn't know what to do to help. I excused myself and went off in the corner where I cried out, 'God, I don't believe in You, but this child and I are in trouble. Please help me!' I can't explain it, there was no voice, no vision, but immediately I knew what to do. I did it and the child lived.

"I finally had a bar mizvah at 13-plus-50. If I had known all the work involved, I wouldn't have tried it, but it went very well. I now believe there is a God utterly beyond human understanding. All religions are man's attempt to understand this God. The old testament is a perfect example of the evolution of man's idea of God."

David Goldstein, poet, philosopher, musician.

16 YOU FIND MORE JOY IN YOUR FAITH

"One of my greatest things is more ministry in our church. We can give a lot of time to the church now. I'm the church secretary but this goes much beyond that. I think I've enjoyed life more in the last ten or twelve years than all the rest put together. There's a special grace in every ten years and my favorite is now. My word is enjoy, every day is important, every year is important and I'll live every one of them 'til I go, either sitting at my desk at the church or out on the golf course.

"I used to be a worrier but not anymore. Now I take things as they come and am grateful every day for all the goodness and richness we have. I give that credit to the Lord, not my age."
Dale Allen.

"Several years ago I took a class on co-dependency that I didn't get all the way through because I had to go help my daughter. It was really good for me as I learned that with all my independence, I like to be in control. I'm sure I did that with my kids. Now I see where it applies to my faith. I kind of want to tell God what to do, not sit back and wait for Him to do things.

Good thing we have such a gracious God."
Charlotte Murphy, on some steps in faith, viewed from her single life.

"It's easier to go to church now, maybe because I have time during the week to do the chores I had to do over the weekend. I seem to enjoy it more too. Not so much hell-fire and damnation."
J.S., who enjoys building things.

"I love to tell my grandchildren, and other children too, about spiritual things. Is it because I understand more or that I have more time to think about God and heaven myself? I don't know, but I wish I had shared more with my children."
Bessie Logan, who shares her faith.

"I've been a Christian all my life but now I know that I really, really, really am Christ's. And I know that's where my joy comes from."
Kristen Johnson Ingram.

"I find myself thinking more about eternal life now. Is it because I'm getting closer to the end and I want life to continue?"
Harvey Kolstad, who's found new creativity in his retirement.

"I don't see religion as separate from daily life. God doesn't know the distinction between secular and sacred."

Dr. Cecil Osborne, who lives an integrated life that just gets more enjoyable.

"Religion is more relaxed now so I'm not afraid to go to church. Some of those preachers used to terrify me. Today the services pick me up rather than beat me down. I like the way that church is also part of my social life now. It's something my wife and I do together."

Oliver Graham.

17 YOU BECOME ~~FREE~~ TO SET YOUR OWN SCHEDULE

"I relish lying in bed on those winter mornings when snow covers the ground while others get their cars out and skid off to work."
Marjorie Love, retired corporate accountant.

"It seems all my life I've been at some place at a certain time on someone else's schedule. Be at work at eight, church on Sunday at a certain time, get up, get dressed. Now, in my 60s, it's about time to do a bit of my own schedule. Take a little more control instead of being constantly driven by someone or something. I want to be less structured, but there's plenty I want to do."
Phil Oestricher, soon to be retired.

"My bed feels awfully good after six in the morning. I really appreciate not having to get up and hustle off to a job or get someone else off."
Helen Bryant, loving retirement living.

"I can take a nap in the afternoon if I want."
Harvey Kolstad.

18 YOU HAVE FREEDOM FROM JOB RESPONSIBILITIES

"Growing older has its virtues, such as not having to make job choices anymore. No more nagging feeling that you should be doing something you're not doing — or should have done something you didn't do. No more anxiety about whether you'll make a good impression on your new boss, new client . . . "
Victor Gold, from his column in **The Washington,** *June 1990.*

"I appreciate not having deadlines anymore, unless I set them myself. I'm not responsible for others in the business world, the hiring and firing, checking to make sure everyone got their jobs done. I don't miss any of that at all."
An ex-businessman.

"I was a librarian in Long Beach, California when I retired and my first freedom was not having to get on that bus every morning at 8:00. I was more than ready to retire; I wanted to travel, to go places I'd never seen. I walked out of that life and into another, only this time I was doing it on my time, on my terms. I planned a kind of working retirement, taking my skills with me because I had heard that librarians were wanted, needed and accepted all over the world. I could see much of the world this way, but I went to Alaska and that's as far as I got. I fell in love with it. My assignment lasted several years as I worked in a small college library. I always had my fingers in something, then my elbows and right up to my neck. But I couldn't resist the lure of Alaska and made many trips back, always working in the libraries. But free. I loved it. I could come and go as I wanted, so now I loved the work, the people and the land even more."

Hazel Van Marter, who had a marvelous time with her second life.

YOU HAVE THE FREEDOM TO GO WHERE YOU'RE NEEDED

"My years of widowhood have given me the freedom to go where I'm needed, for my family, friends and church. I love being with my grandkids, so when they need me — I go. Seems that sometimes I live in my car. Good thing I love to drive. I work at keeping old friendships open too.

"My freedom makes it easier. I don't have to consult another person and set my schedule around his likes and needs. One thing I realize as I get older, family and friends and, of course, my faith, are the most important things in this world."

Charlotte Murphy.

"Since I retired and my second husband died, I've had the freedom to help out my family and others when they called. When my granddaughter had cancer and needed some home health care, I could go do that. I can get another granddaughter off to school when she needs me. Sometimes I'm asked to check on the pets when one of my daughters is out of town. Everyone can't always come to my house, so I can go to theirs. Like when an elderly friend of mine needed a break from caring for her husband who had Alzheimer's. Al and I did just fine. My nursing background comes in handy, but most of the time, I just love to be there for my family and friends."

Thelma Sommerseth, retired but not rusting out.

20 YOU CARE LESS WHAT OTHERS THINK

"What people think about you doesn't matter anymore. It's not guaranteed in old age but you can't get there before then."
Sandy Dengler, who loves to make people laugh.

"As I get older and build a new life in a second marriage, I have the freedom to decorate my house the way I want. I've chosen furnishings and art work because they make me feel good, not because of what's fashionable. I don't care about the current colors or prints or textures. I want a house that's a home and says 'Come and be comfortable here.' "
Sally Stuart, feeling the freedom.

"For years I've worked with young people in our church and I love every minute of it. This is the fun of getting older, and — I used to laugh at this — now I can hug the boys as much as the girls and nobody pays any attention. You've got a really good conscience and you just enjoy lovin' them. All of us need all the hugs we can get."
Irene McWhorter, who's mothered many a needy kid.

21 YOU CAN FINALLY DRESS AS YOU WISH

"I don't have to be stylish anymore, you know, the hemline the right length, fashionable clothes for your job. You can wear clothes that are comfortable, not the dresses, gloves and hats that I used to wear. I felt real freedom when they let us wear slack suits which were wonderful in my job of finding things in the files."
Mazie Maxey, retired auditor.

"I don't have to wear high heels anymore, I can wear flats."
Ruby MacDonald, writer.

"You know white anklets look bad, and you don't care — you wear them anyway."
Aldean Rasmussen, who keeps her age a secret.

"Now I can dress for me. I don't have to impress anyone else. Even when I work with those in the poor community, I can wear my suits and heels if I want and because I'm comfortable, they are too."
Dr. Effie Chow, founder of The East/West Academy for Healing Arts.

WARNING

When I am an old woman, I shall wear purple
With a red hat which doesn't go, and doesn't
   suit me.
And I shall spend my pension on brandy and
   summer gloves
And satin sandals, and say we've no money for
   butter.

I shall sit down on the pavement when I'm tired
And gobble up samples in shops and press
   alarm bells
And run my stick along the public railings
And make up for the sobriety of my youth.
I shall go out in my slippers in the rain
And pick flowers from other people's gardens
And learn to spit.

You can wear terrible shirts and grow more fat
And eat three pounds of sausage at a go
Or only bread and pickles for a week
And hoard pens and pencils and beermats and
   things in boxes.

But now we must have clothes that keep us dry
And pay our rent and not swear in the street
And set a good example for our children.
We must have friends to dinner and read the
   papers.
But maybe I ought to practise a little now?
So people who know me are not too shocked
   and surprised
When suddenly I am old, and start to wear
   purple.

                    Jenny Joseph

"When I was younger and so poor I had to sew everything, the latest styles were very important to me. Now when I can buy what I want, I wear what is comfortable. I buy quality and then if the jacket is old, who knows? It still looks and feels good. Besides, someone else can always have a better jacket than you, more jewelry. But I've learned to be comfortable with what I have and not reach for more than what I am comfortable with."
Jade Snow Wong, who dresses for herself.

"I'd rather have comfy sweats than a new fur coat."
Sally Knauss.

"It's great to give up ties except for 'suit' occasions."
Carl Barclay, happy in golf clothes.

22

YOU CAN SAY OR DO AS YOU PLEASE

"You can do what you want to do without being embarrassed about what other people think."
Mazie Maxey, artist.

"It all comes down to what you feel inside. If you like yourself, then you don't have to worry so much what others think. You can say what you like. You can have and enjoy the child-like qualities within. Now, not childish, but child-like. Things like enjoying dancing around, exuberance, laughing, all the traits of that wonderful child within. You can live for you, you no longer have to impress others."
Dr. Effie Chow, who loves to dance, laugh and sing.

"As I've gotten older, I've become somewhat of a guru in my field. Pilots and engineers come to me for answers. With that, I've come to be able to recognize what is important and what isn't. You know pilots are a pretty egotistical bunch, especially those from the military. I used to be somewhat entertained by these arrogant, don't-care-who-they-step-on, aggressive people. Now I find I don't have any tolerance for them, in fact, if I can sabotage them once in awhile, I'll do it. And I enjoy it. I'm quite happy to tell them exactly what I think. Guess that's part of not caring so much what other people think. Fifteen years ago I would have been more reticent, more career conscious, chosen my words a little more carefully. Now I'm paid for my opinion, so I give it."

Phil Oestricher, pilot/engineer, guru.

"I'm not afraid to say what I think anymore. You can be outspoken and claim senility."

Sandy Dengler, a writer from the beach retreat.

"If I could speak at one time to all senior Americans, I'd tell them to forget their age and do exactly what they feel like doing. It all comes down to attitude. Excitement is what really keeps you going."

*Bob Hope, in **Old Age Isn't For Sissies** by Art Linkletter.*

"You can speak your mind without editorializing. I've always said that the two best interviewees are from ages four to ten and those over 65. They always say exactly what they think. The children don't know what they're saying and the older people don't care."

Art Linkletter, author, interviewer extraordinaire.

"We bring out in the open and talk about so many

things now that would never have been mentioned 50 years ago. Things like child abuse, battered wives, alcohol within the family. These now are admitted, talked about, recognized as real problems. And with the openness can come healing and healthy growth."

Ruth Stafford Peale, wife, mother, full of concern for the hurting. While she lives in New York, she calls the world her home.

"It's fun sometimes to say 'I told you so.' I try not to do it often but . . ."

Flora Euller, who at 92 has earned the right to say what she thinks.

"We always tell our kids, don't speak to strangers, but older women can talk to anyone. No one's going to accuse you of flirting, you can just jabber along."

Hazel May Rue, who has talked with some pretty interesting people in her time.

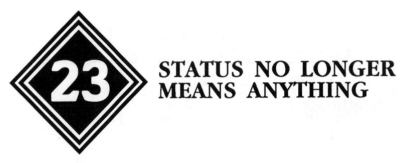

23 STATUS NO LONGER MEANS ANYTHING

"You realize true value comes from inside, not from all the toys you collected."
A retired plumber.

"I've had it all, the big house, help, fancy cars, my husband's name known so therefore mine, shopping at the expensive stores. I enjoyed it, but that wasn't where I came from. It all had to do with my husband and his name. My younger life was simpler and I'm ready to go back to that. Stuff didn't buy happiness. It's time to be me."
Kathleen Harries, an explorer.

"When you move into a housing tract in your early married years, it is really easy to get caught up in the keep-up race, even very subtly. When the kids down the street get a new bike, your child wants one. Clothes should be a certain brand. You want your house to look nice, too. But even though we weren't status die-hards, I can see a difference now. . . . I refuse to buy something for someone else's opinion. Now I want ease and comfort."
From a woman who's status-free and loves it.

TOO LATE

YOU LEARN THE IMPORTANCE OF EXERCISE TO REBUILD OR MAINTAIN HEALTH

Wendy Kohrt, an associate professor of medicine at Washington University in St. Louis, recently completed a five-year study in which 110 sedentary men and women from ages 60-71 were put through a rigorous exercise program. By the first year's end, all were exercising 40-50 minutes a day, five days a week at heart rates of 80 to 90 percent of their maximum heart rate. All improved their cardiovascular function 20 to 25 percent, the same improvement noted in studies of young people. Muscle size was tripled with weight training.

All were walking 15-20 miles a week by the end of the study, some running and jogging.

"When I joined the [above] program I told them I might walk that far but never run. By the end, I ran six miles. That makes you feel real good about yourself. Now life is a smorgasbord. I'm not afraid to try something and if I like it, I go back for more."
Clara Wolff, participant in the exercise study.

"No one's ever run the New York Marathon at 100 and I'd like to be the first to do it. My life insurance was canceled because I was such a bad risk and my doctor said not to strain myself. But I started walking instead. My hours of exercise erased years of physical atrophy. Now I jump on a trampoline, walk, run, box and I'd like to try tennis. I'm glad I'm 92 years young, not 70 years old. My one regret? My doctor didn't live long enough to cheer me on."
Noel Johnson, in USA **Weekend** *1991.*

"How would you like to have a good body, great health and move like a dancer at age 65? I bought a paperback called the *Royal Canadian Air Force Plan for Physical Fitness* and started the work-outs in 1962. It took 15 minutes, three or four times a week to keep my measurements at 36-26-36. What else could I have done with that amount of time that would ever be more worthwhile as I raised a family and had a professional career? I'm a mature single now and find that men are interested in the same thing they always were."
Erma Giddings, writer, volunteer.

"I know how to knit but I never do it. I can't sit still that long. I love to read but again, you have to sit still. For a good book, I force myself. But I love to be out and going. Walking, even in the misty weather of Oregon, is one of my chief pleasures. We have a golf course right down the street with a walking path all around it. You'll find me there almost every day I'm at home. Otherwise I'm traveling."

At 88 Hazel Stout can walk most people into the ground. But she says she hasn't made it to the top of Mt. Hood — yet.

"Dr. Peale and I are in our 90s and walk half a mile to a mile every day. While we've always been walkers, it's only lately there's been such an emphasis on exercise. So many people as they grow older, if they don't realize the importance of walking or exercising, somehow become very sedentary — then you can't do anything but sit."

Ruth Stafford Peale, who still travels the globe.

"The whole thing is maintenance. If you want to stay trim, keep your stomach in, your boobs up and your arms tight, there's a more relaxed way of working out. I didn't do my tape [exercise video] to win awards. It's like me — kind of unsteady and keeps moving along."

*Debbie Reynolds, in **Woman's Day**, April 10, 1990.*

"I took swimming lessons after I retired so now I can swim laps, which really helps keep my knees working. My kick isn't the greatest but the water is good therapy anyway."

Thelma Sommerseth, who loves warm water but only finds it in the pool near her home.

"I'm learning to cook healthy and exercise better so this good time of life will be extended or just be better while it lasts."

Aris Painter, executive nurse.

Hulda Crooks climbed Mount Whitney for the first time at age 66. In the last 26 years she's made the trip 23 times.

"It's never too late to improve your health," she said. "Many people are afraid of hurting themselves if they do anything active. Others think they don't need it. But if anyone needs activity, it's older people."

*Hulda Crooks, a California climber, in **Modern Maturity**.*

25 YOU LEARN TO LISTEN TO YOUR BODY TALK

"You learn to see your health and body in a holistic way. We're all one piece, not an arm or a head or the sinuses. When part of my body complains, the whole is affected. So I try to take care of all of me, from brain to bottoms of my feet and from the inside to the outside. Sure have learned a lot over the years."

Pat Rushford, who gave up nursing to write.

"I'm trying to learn to do this. I've taken this body of mine for granted for too many years and sadly, the way most bodies respond is by screaming with pain. When the pain hits, we listen. Now I try to respond to twinges, to sluggish feelings, you know, that I'm-not-quite-up-to-par-but-no-idea-what's-wrong feeling.

"I've found that taking three or four deep breaths, preferably out of doors, standing straighter to breathe deeply, and maybe doing some shoulder shrugs is marvelous medicine. Singing, laughing, anything that gets the blood flowing a bit faster helps.

"Simple stretches like arms to the ceiling, hugging both my shoulders, (hugs are an antidote for anything in my book) all seem to make me feel more alert — and happier. I seem to hear a pleased sigh from my body, too."

L.S., learning to listen.

"Whenever the old body startes to twinge from cold or dampness, the best antidote is a trip to a warmer, dryer, clime."

Libby Hall, author and traveler who takes her business with her.

"Whenever I get little aches, I know the best thing to do is exercise. When I *really* get smart, I'll exercise *first.*"

P.B., a little smarter.

26

YOU DISCOVER LAUGHTER IS NOT ONLY FUN BUT KEEPS YOU HEALTHY

Laugh your way to health:
DeKalb General Hospital offers unusual treatment for patients who seem to be giving up. It's off to the humor room for a few hours. The cheerful room lacks medical equipment; the stock is televisions and VCR's with a library of old movies like Laurel and Hardy, W.C. Fields, funny television shows and radio shows of Red Skelton, Groucho Marx, Abbott and Costello. Even hospitals are beginning realize the importance of laughter and learning to laugh.

Besides improving communication, hearty laughter eases muscular tension, helps the respiratory system and increases oxygen in the blood. Therefore patients think more clearly. Not a bad prescription for anyone.
From an article in AARP Bulletin.

"You can't do better for your physical being than laugh. That's the greatest relaxant of all time. It make Valium look like a placebo."
Bob Hope makes sure the entire world laughs.

"Humor should be as natural as breathing. Look closely, you'll find something keenly human and discernibly humorous about everyone.

"Lighten up and smile, then let yourself laugh. Laughter is the cheapest prescription in town, but often is rarer than the Kohinoor diamond. So cultivate your sense of humor. You need it. The world around you needs it."

*Malcolm Boyd, in You and I column in **Modern Maturity**.*

"One of the things I like about my life now is that I laugh more than I cry. I've always been cheerful and laughed a lot but didn't realize how important it was. There's a physiological mechanism in laughter that helps the brain create endorphins which can be compared to morphine but are much stronger. These endorphins are both pain killers and mood elevators. I used to laugh without knowing what I was doing. Now I consciously choose laughter because it's fun and healthy too."

Dr. Lendon H. Smith, retired pediatrician.

YOU LEARN THAT CRISIS CAN FORCE YOU TO LIVE A HEALTHIER LIFESTYLE

"I had a heart attack and by-pass surgery that helped change my outlook on life. You come out of the surgery and the hospital depressed, but after talking with others, you learn to live one day at a time. I probably feel better now than I have in 15 years. With modern medicine, having a by-pass isn't much more difficult than having your appendix out."

Bob Allen, small business owner.

"After my first heart attack and by-pass at 42, I tried to change things, quit smoking, no red meat, low fat but then I slipped back into the old habits. Eleven years later I was back at the hospital for a repeat. When the doctor finished, he said, 'I don't *ever* want to see you here again.'

"So I became a good boy. My wife feeds me wisely and carefully, I'm on the treadmill every day, keep my weight down, no smoking, little drinking and I don't mind. Back the first time, the by-pass didn't mean anything. They fixed it. But this time, guess I realized my own mortality. The surgery took eleven hours, seven of which was spent cutting through the scar tissue. The recovery was a mess and I don't want to go through that again. I don't want to die out of sheer stupidity. So while I've had a good life, I'd like to keep it going longer."

Jim Bosley, TV talkshow host and weatherman.

"I was an alcoholic with a bleeding ulcer, and was in and out of the hospital. On my last trip, after I had hemorrhaged pretty badly, the nurse left my chart on my bedside table when she walked out of the room — I think now it was on purpose! My chart read 'alcoholic - terminal.' I called Alcoholics Anonymous from the hospital, and someone came to see me that day. I never had another drink, and I've taken good care of myself ever since."

Carl Barclay, who told this story in his early 80s.

"Health is a golden halo that we all wear but only see when we're sick."

Dr. Herbert Schwartz, quoting "Hippocrates or Socrates or some such."

TOO LATE

28 ◆ YOU LEARN TO TAKE RESPONSIBILITY FOR YOUR OWN HEALTH

"I was doing everything right and still I had a second heart attack. These are some of the things I've learned. I'm more selective about the speeches I agree to make. My columns carry a stronger take-care-of-yourself component. I've stopped playing the 'I win-you lose' game with my wife. Winning isn't so important — what matters is being close. I frequently phone my two sons and share what's going on inside of me. I make time for friends — even impromptu. I'm more at peace with myself. In general, I'm less demanding, less impatient, because I realize that, once you've arrived, getting there first turns out not to mean so much after all."

Darrell Sifford, in **New Choices***, February. 1991*

One physician advised his high-risk heart patients to learn:
1. Don't sweat the small stuff.
2. It's all small stuff
David Sobel, MD, MPH, in **The Healing Brain**

"I decided many years ago that I was going to live to be a hundred," Bob Hope said. "My grandfather was one month short of a hundred when he passed away, so I've got a pretty good start as far as heredity. I concentrate on staying healthy. I've developed a routine I never digress from. It keeps my motor running smoothly. It was my idea, not a doctor's and I know I found a pattern that works. It includes eating right, vitamins, exercise, enough rest and cut out the smokes and back on the booze."

For Bob Hope's complete plan see **The Saturday Evening Post**, *October '81*

"One of the good things in my life is that if I don't feel well, I know what to do about it. If I get a chest cough, I take extra vitamin A. Extra C for a cold. A doctor out of Spokane, who's a strong advocate of vitamin and mineral supplements, says to go by the smell system. If a vitamin or mineral in its pure state smells good, you need it. If it smells bad, you don't need it. It really works. Apparently that's why your nose is in the place it is."

Dr. Lendon H. Smith, who has found that we are just a bag of chemicals and if you are taking the right stuff in the right proportions, you'll feel better.

"This is the way I approach life. What is it I need and how can I get it? Then I do just that. I go out and get what I need so I can function. Like now I know I need to eat every four hours and no matter where I travel or what I'm doing, I make sure that need is met. I'm the only one responsible for taking care of me."

Pat Smith, 53, who learned through experience to cope.

"My associate at the Pauling Center, Dr. Rath, and I believe we have discovered a way to control heart disease by earlier detection. We've learned that low levels of vitamin C, ascorbic acid, allows a build-up of lipoprotien A as it repairs weakened blood vessel walls. Too much of this lipoprotien A in the blood is an indication that a person is a candidate for future heart problems. A simple blood screening can detect this and increased vitamin C, several grams a day can be a prevention. We're quite excited about this. Dr. Rath has been in Washington, D.C. presenting a paper on our finding."

Dr. Linus Carl Pauling, who is still doing research at 90.

Health maintenance is the primary function of the brain, not rational thought, language or poetry. Research has shown that visualization (imagining your white blood cells are like sharks patrolling your body is search of germs, for example), relaxation training, or even watching a funny movie can produce measurable changes in the immune system.

YOU LEARN THAT YOU CAN OVERCOME ADDICTIONS

"I finally know me, like me, and live one day at a time. I am a recovering alcoholic with eight years sobriety. I would be dead by now if it weren't for AA, Alcoholics Anonymous. I was never a falling down drunk but I was never honest with myself either. I drank — I had to. That's the difference between an alcoholic and others. I had to. Now I can make choices in my life, I can explore who I really am and I like the woman inside me. I have no patience for those who judge, those who keep others out, especially when they claim to be Christian."

An AA member.

"Our freedom is of a different sort. My wife and I have been AA and Al-Anon members for 13 years. Every family can seek the kind of help that is available through 12-step programs.

"This has been a period of tremendous growth for us and I think it plays a large part in our present sense of fulfillment and gratitude."

An AA member.

ALWAYS
DID

30 YOU BECOME SMART ENOUGH TO LEARN FROM OTHER PEOPLE'S PROBLEMS

"Since I worked in the medical field of blood disorders, (leukemia, hemophilia, etc.) for children, I see health as extremely important. When I see all the suffering I want to make sure my family does all it can to be healthy. No one can be more grateful than I for the health of my entire family."

Herbert Schwartz, retired pediatric M.D. from Stanford.

"As I hear stories of what people have endured, I gain a tremendous respect for them, for their will to survive. I begin to believe that anyone can become whole again as I see others do exactly that. And as I've seen others and kept on with my own process, I know now that I too will make it."

Grace Prochnow, who is now sharing her beliefs with others on the way to healing.

"One of the things I learned from watching other people's mistakes was the need to clear things up with your loved ones before they die. I heard so many 'if only's' and 'I wish I had's' that I determined that wouldn't happen with me. My father and I didn't have a terribly wonderful relationship for years but now that his health is failing drastically, I decided I had to make the first move. I began telling him I love him. I kept repeating the words, joined with loving and caring actions, until one day, he had to tell me back. After the first time, it was so much easier for him. It would have been so simple to not have initiated the loving, to have carried my self-righteousness to the end, but this is much healthier — and freeing. For both of us."

Kathleen Harries, who has wisdom beyond her years.

"I have always tried to learn from the experiences of others because it can save me misery and pain. As I grow older, my wisdom opens my eyes wider, especially in the ways to grow older. By comparing what others have or have not done regarding aging, I learn what I must do to grow older productively."

A woman in the know.

YOU NO LONGER HAVE TO WORRY ABOUT PREGNANCY

"Not worrying about pregnancy is one of the greatest things about post-menopause. I know modern women don't have to worry about it these days, but we did. And I know many younger women worry in spite of all the new-fangled preventions they have on the market. It's too easy to slip up. But I don't worry anymore."

Sandy Dengler, an author who has followed her ranger husband around the country.

"The first 45 years I worried about birth control which stole away spontaneity. After menopause came a new sexual freedom. Sex could be spontaneous and worry-free of pregnancy, which I believe is one of the things Browning meant in his famous line, '. . . the last of life for which the first was made.' "

A 60+ woman who loves her continuing sexuality.

"I asked the 'What's good' question to an office full of women, and the answer that kept recurring was 'You don't have to worry about getting pregnant'!"

Alice Musgrove, who serves through real estate.

 **YOUR BRAIN IMPROVES WITH AGE**

Everyone knows that brain cells die as we age but the ones that remain help us get smarter. They develop more synapsis, the threadlike connectors from cell to cell, so that more bits of information that come in have places to stick, thus increasing our intelligence.

From the findings of Dr. William T. Greenough, Professor of Psychology and chairman of a program in neuro-science of behavior at the University of Illinois.

"I am reflecting on this strange and awesome brain of mine. The longer I live, the more it seems to have a life of its own. I always thought my brain belonged to me — was my servant as it were. Now I find that it has its own priorities, eccentricities and schedules. I have two choices: I can fight it, knowing I can't win, or I can go along for the ride, wherever it may take me."

*Eda Leshan, from **It's Better To Be Over the Hill Than Under It.***

"I've found that I have difficulty pulling names out of my memory bank. Well, of course, my memory bank is a pretty big one so as far as hunting around for something, it may take longer. This difficulty sets in rapidly after 70 or 85 or so. Sometimes I have to think for several seconds when years ago only a fraction of a second was needed. But my mind brings it up. If I'm giving a lecture, sometimes I say, 'Well, I'll have to tell you that name later.'

"While my recall takes more time, my reasoning power is as good as ever, possibly even better, I'm not sure. I continue to do original, novel scientific work. I continue to write and publish in the scientific and medical fields, lecture and try to figure out answers to questions on the 'why' of this world."

Dr. Linus Carl Pauling, whose thinking has made incredible differences in our world.

"K. Warner Schaire, Ph.D., professor of human development at Pennsylvania State University, says that the overall thinking skills of a 55-year-old are almost always markedly superior to those of a 25-year-old. He has shown that a challenged brain never quits learning."

From I Dare You! How to Stay Young Forever by Lucile Bogue.

33 YOU DEVELOP WISDOM

"Mentally, the central value of age is wisdom. Wisdom results from a huge backdrop of accumulated memories and experiences that bring unique perspectives to new problems."

*From **Aging Well** by James F. Fries, M.D.*

"I know I've become wiser with age and it's obvious in the little things. You get sort of a knowing, it comes from within. You're more at peace with yourself and others. Little things don't seem to mean to much to you anymore. Your house doesn't have to be so immaculate anymore, other things, people, Bible study are more important to me now. Friendships and doing things for others are more important. I could never do as much as I wanted before and now I have the time to do so.

"As a nurse I was always in the helping others but now I get to see the fruits of what I do. Then it was a physical caring, now my life is more a spiritual caring. It all goes back to time and maybe looking for the right things."

Elaine Aspelund, who has found the wisdom of time.

"I've worked with older people in an Area Agency on Aging. It made me realize, 'That's you further down the road.' If you need to make changes in yourself, you better get on it. That takes wisdom and persistence."

Pauline Goodrich, 59, who's getting on with life.

"Through the years I've gotten smarter, wiser. I know a tremendous amount that I can now capitalize on."

Gail Denham, a writer.

34 YOU BECOME MORE FORGIVING

"You know, my brother and I had a big fight years ago and we didn't speak to each other for years. Now I can hardly even remember what it was all about. I just know it was all his fault since he's the most bull-headed, stubborn guy you ever want to meet. I swore up and down I'd never forgive him, even if he came begging.

"But a few years ago, I was 69 then, I got to missing him so bad it was like a knife in my belly. I'd think back on us as kids and the fun we had. I'd see other brothers and sisters having a great time telling tall tales on each other. One day I just got on the phone and called him up. I cried and he cried. Forgiving isn't really so bad, even if you have to make the first move. Sure glad I did. Now we visit each other a couple of times a year and talk on the phone a lot. . . . Not sure I would have done this when I was younger, but man, am I glad we're back together.

James Addison, a man of courage and a big heart.

"[When you are older] I think you realize how much you will lose if you don't forgive — you can lose a relationship, peace of mind, and even your health if you let yourself continue to be angry. Literally, life is too short!"
P.B.

"I guess you could call it forgiving, or maybe it's learning to live with the times, but it's really hard for me when people, especially my children and grand-children, live together without being married. I know if I carried a grudge, I'd never see them, so I accept the situation and love them anyway."
Claribell Christopherson, a forgiver.

"Rearing children gives one plenty of practice in forgiving."
A mother in the know.

YOU BECOME
MORE INTUITIVE

Intuition is a natural mental ability, strongly associated with experience which Roy Rowan, author of *The Intuitive Manager*, believes heightens through our 50s and 60s.

"By that age we've accumulated a lot of life experience, a knowledge of other people, a sense of ourselves. Most important, we have both the wisdom and the courage to act on our instincts.

"It seems that the older we get, the greater the data bank of knowledge our intuition has to draw on. Another researcher says that 'intuition is what the brain knows how to do when we leave it alone.'

"So listen to that inner sense. And once you have a flash of insight, write it down. It can vanish as fast as it came. Listen, you earned it."

From an article in New Choices, May 1991.

"I've become more intuitive. I don't think our intuition changes. I think we are born with what we've been allotted and it's up to us to develop it. Intuition is a gift that allow me a protection and an awareness that I would miss greatly if I didn't have it.

"I used to have gut feelings and I would do all I

could to ignore them. Now, expecially in my work as a therapist, I do a lot of things in my sessions that are directly from my gut. They have nothing to do with the rules and experiences of other therapists and studies, but it works, especially in art therapy.

"I find and use my intuition too in relationships with some of my friends and my daughter. I always knew when she was in trouble and have learned to call a friend when her names comes to mind insistently. I'm always glad when I listen to these promptings and I've been sorry when I didn't. Guess I've learned to listen more and more."

Gail Grundon.

"My intuition hasn't changed, but it's certainly grown and mostly that's because I've learned to listen to it. There are mistakes in my life that I wouldn't have made if I'd listened to my intuition. I'm very sensitive to people's feelings and how they are going to react. Sometimes I can tell you how someone is going to react when I make a phone call, and it's not just people I know well. I can walk into a room and my intuition will turn on full force, sometimes making me feel I want out of there.

"My sense of intuition helps me in my job because I am so sensitive to other people's feelings. It also helps me personally by keeping me from getting excited about things that I know will pass."

Betty Zarn, who assists handicapped people in living situations.

YOU KNOW YOU CAN ENDURE HARDSHIP AND TRAGEDY — EVEN THE DEATH OF A LOVED ONE

"In all the hard spots in life, I've learned you can be bitter or better."
Kathleen Fuller, who's learned a lot of resilience.

"There are days since my middle-aged son committed suicide that I wonder what I did wrong, how I'll keep going and then I look around and see someone who needs some help and the first thing you know, I've worked myself right out of it."
Dollie Root, a victorious griever.

"I probably have a different view of freedom than most people. I spent six years as a guest of the Vietnamese at the Hanoi Hilton in Saigon. I endured torture and deprivation of every kind. To live, you had to reach deep inside your soul and find those values you were willing to live and die by. I learned that I can endure, that perseverance is a virtue beyond measure and that friends are God's greatest gift to humanity."
Retired Navy Capt. Eugene B. "Red" McDaniel, president and founder of the American Defense Institute.

"There is so much that is new in my life, that I find myself full of energy. The days fly by. Suddenly I realize that I have not cried all week. I realize that I am enjoying life — and then I feel guilty. But not very. There is no reason I should."

Dr. Joyce Brothers, from her book **Widowed**.

"After a sad divorce that ended a marriage of 20 years, I knew I had two choices: I could either be angry, depressed and miserable — or I could make the most out of the rest of my life."

From a woman happy in a new business and a new marriage.

YOU BECOME
MORE ASSERTIVE

"One of the best things to me [about growing older] is that you really know yourself, what you are capable of doing. You no longer have to wonder how you will do. You know that you can go out and learn a new skill if you need to, like if you've had to make a career change. You just set about doing what you need to do."

Pauline Goodrich, who's conquered several careers and now holds a high position in a large city service.

"I'm a fighter. I've learned how to adjust to my three-story house surroundings so I can stay here. I'll do the best I can and the best I know and if anybody doesn't like it, they can go to the devil. On the whole I am very happy with myself."

Flora Euller, who at 92 has earned the right to speak her mind.

"All my early married life, I fitted myself into my husband's lifestyle, his expectations, his name and family. As I got older and smarter and the feminist movement came along, I worked to develop assertiveness. I began to have the freedom to voice my own ideas and opinions and to disagree with him when I felt it necessary. He didn't like it, not at all.

"I believed that to be true to me and to become the me that was hiding inside, I needed to think for myself, begin to have a life of my own. I even, heaven forbid, mentioned that I thought women gave up their identity when they took on their husband's name. It hasn't been easy, but one can be assertive and not bitchy, speak up without attacking others. To me, assertive means thinking enough of oneself to expect others to respect you, to treat you fairly and to recognize you as an individual — with value."

Kathy Harries, who loves to see herself in her daughter, who is also assertive.

"I've become more assertive as I've grown older because age has endowed me with more confidence in myself, stronger values and the power to stand up and fight for what I believe. Therefore, I seldom allow people to walk over me as I did when I was younger."

A gracious woman, but strong.

38 ◇ YOU FINALLY BEGIN TO KNOW YOURSELF

"After all these years I finally know myself. I've figured out what part is parental influence, what came from my husband. I know what makes me tick and I understand what is really important. People can't really know themselves until around 50."

A woman in communications.

"I no longer have to prove or improve myself. Like why tat when I'd rather crochet? Is it really best to do the laundry on Monday like my mother did? Now I do things because I want to, not because I ought to."

Sandy Dengler, who gave up trying to conform and is richer for it.

"I know myself. I've lived with myself for a hell of a long time, so if I don't know myself by now, I'm never going to."

*Katherine Hepburn, **Saturday Evening Post,** January 1992.*

"Getting to know myself is a lengthy process that

started in agony before I turned 50 but became pleasant in the last two or three years. What I didn't know before is that I have within me the ability to create. Fear held me back before so I didn't try. When I draw, I draw from within, it is me and very hard to give away or sell. In fact, I don't. My drawing reveals a lot of turbulence and emotion and thus has taught me about who I really am. Now I'm not bound by trying to figure out what others want of me and using all my energy to fulfill their desires. I am free and my drawing shows me that."

Grace Prochnow, who sings freedom's song with joy.

YOU LIKE THE "ME" INSIDE

"No matter how many people have loved us in our lives, the love we need most of all is the love we give ourselves. It's the springboard to a creative and meaningful and fulfilling life when we are alone."

*Eda LeShan, from her book **It's Better to be Over the Hill than Under It.***

"I had to discover the 'me' before I could like the 'me'. . . and I could like me once I got through all the crap, the shame I had brought with me from childhood. I like the fun I have with my creative part. I can be a basket case and go work in the pottery room and come out refreshed. I really like me."

Grace Prochnow, who endured so she can now enjoy.

"One of my favorite Bible verses is one of the hardest for me. It says '. . . to love the Lord your God with all your heart and soul and mind . . . and your neighbor as yourself.' The hard part was learning to love and even like myself. That 'me' that lives inside where no one else can see. But now I see that she/me is a pretty special person."

L.S., confessions of growing up.

YOU HAVE LESS NEED TO CONTROL OTHERS

"My need to control others has pretty well disappeared. Through AA I learned to let go, but it's just been gradually over the years I've learned I can't control others. Thinking you can is just a head trip, but the real gut level understanding is easier now. Where before I had to kind of work at it, now I don't. It used to be if they weren't doing it my way, then they weren't doing it right. That changed a lot after I got in AA, but then I had to work at it. Now control doesn't matter anymore."

Dick Cavnar, who's given up trying to control others and is much happier with himself.

"I see giving up that need to control others as a task of our maturity, not something that one gains just because they turned 50. While it would be healthier to do so younger, usually we need the wisdom of years to make us want to. The opposite of controlling is letting go, and of course, the ultimate in letting go is dying, so I see this as a preparation for death. To the extent we go through this letting go of control, we're freed up from the fear of dying and so free to really live the last part of our lives.

"When we let go of the control, it improves our relationships with friends and family. Adult children resent being controlled and when you can let go and let them run their own lives, the more you'll have adult/adult relationships. I could see this with my mother. I didn't even dare give a hint that I might be telling her what to do.

"The other thing I see is physiological. When we spend a lot of energy trying to control, our muscles get tight and as we get older, the tension causes arthritis, sore backs, whatever. I'm really grateful I've been learning to let go because I don't need one more ache or pain and I don't want to give them either."

C. Jay Hawkins, who teaches others to let go.

"A big component of the need to control others is the need to have everything done *your* way. I think age and experience teach us, finally, that if it's all done *your* way, the people around you are unhappy, and you, consequently, are unhappy too. What a hard lesson to learn! But I'm getting much better."

P.B., improving slowly.

41 YOU GAIN SELF-CONFIDENCE

"You get a confidence from your experiences. If your life is working at all, if you're having any kind of success, having the courage to do certain things will give you not only knowledge but confidence. You gain that courage by finding out that things aren't really as hard as you first thought.

"I had a friend who, when anyone asked her to do something, always said, 'No problem,' and then she said, 'You just run around figuring out how to do it.' I found it works for me too.

"I learned that sometimes the people who seem the most confident are really bluffing and that was an enormous comfort, a freeing kind of thing.

"When I was to take my masters exam I was scared to death, sure I would fail it. But then I realized, if I failed the exam, that was a failure of knowledge. If I didn't take it, that was a failure of courage, and that is a problem. So you just do it and you survive and your confidence grows."

Pat Smith, editor at a university press.

"I've learned I'm not the shy person I thought I was at 18. I know I can try new things, work at jobs and do a good job with what I've got. I'm pretty positive. With all our moves, we've learned to adjust. I don't have time to be unhappy with a move. I'm kinda' the cheerleader around here, for kids, guests at our motel, whoever. I found that I have no trouble at all voicing my opinion, asked for or not and who cares."

Del Voorhees, a happy adventurer.

"I know that one thing I have going for me is that I've built a good self image. That carries you through all kinds of ups and downs. I've learned to stay away from negative people and situations that would be put-downs. All in all, this helps keep me healthy and happy."

Dr. Lendon H. Smith, who's learned to laugh a lot, mostly at himself.

YOU REALIZE YOU ARE NOT DEPENDENT ON OTHERS FOR YOUR HAPPINESS

"I always thought that my happiness came from outside of me, that everything depended upon the situation I was in. Somewhere around 50, I began to realize that I was in charge of my own life. That's a tremendous relief, not only to me but to the people around me. I'm no longer demanding anything from them, I know now that my happiness comes from inside of me.

Kristen Johnson Ingram, philosopher.

"Happiness comes from within. It is a good feeling about yourself and your loved ones. You are content and satisfied with yourself. You may not have accomplished what you wanted to, but that no longer matters. A few months ago I realized I was feeling about as happy as I'd ever been. I was forced to take early retirement from my career company and now I have a job that I really enjoy. I like getting up in the morning again. I like my job. Everything isn't perfect, but I'm happy with where I am."

John George, who understands the secret of happiness.

"We [the women over 60] have always been the gang who could find something to do. We played school and house and store. We had a dozen ways to play hide-and-seek. Remember kick-the-can and punch-the-icebox? We jumped rope, played jacks, made clothes for our Dionne Quintuplet paper dolls. We had our own clubs and organized our own groups to build playhouses or lemonade stands. We could always find something to do. Nobody had to entertain us or bankroll our lifestyle. We thought it out ourselves.

"That woman who thinks she needs money for a cruise in order to be happy is driving her ducks to a poor market . . . we can improve our own lives; make the most of these years of leisure time . . . create that fleeting moment of happiness."

Frances Weaver, from **As Far As I Can See.**

"My happiness comes from within myself. I seek it. I work at it. If I find something I like and I think it would be beneficial for me, then I work towards that goal. I have a lot of faith in God, it's important in my life. Happiness in my case means content within yourself. You have to be happy within your soul. And when you are happy within your soul, then you can give that happiness to others."

Jackie George, whose very voice radiates happiness.

43 YOU REALIZE YOU BELONG TO YOURSELF

"I'm my own person. If I try something new and it fails, I don't feel like I'm a big failure. If I do something and I succeed, it just makes me happier than anything. If I want to go to the library, I do or answer if someone needs me. Now I'm doing the things that make me happy and I think it makes others happy too."
Dollie Root, a grown-up woman.

"I realize I am my own person. This came over a period of time, mostly after I retired as head of the math department at a local college. I worry less and less about what I'm 'supposed' to do. I do what I want. I can now make different statements with my clothes. Like the time I wore pink sneakers to a meeting. Everyone there was about my age and raved about my pink sneakers. I just felt like wearing pink sneakers that day."
Ruth Heintz, Ph.D.

"I'm finally free to be my own person. I don't belong to my husband or my family. I belong to me."
Sarah James.

44 YOU DEVELOP MORE SELF-DISCIPLINE

"One way self-discipline develops is when people become interested in something that gives meaning to their lives, and focus their time and energy on it. Research shows that mental health, and often physical health, is improved when people develop a commitment toward something or someone in addition to themselves. This commitment increases their passion for life."

Muriel James, a living example of self-discipline to benefit others.

"Self-discipline to me, is the power to choose how you are going to handle the things that come up in life. When the hard places come, and they do to everyone, you can choose to go to pieces, or with the self-control you've developed through the years, work things out in a constructive way.

"We've just had a situation in our family that proves the point. One of the family members has chosen to go in a direction we're not happy with. Now I could sit and visualize all the terrible things that could happen to her, worry and stew and fret myself into a total disaster. But would that help? No!

And I have the power to choose to turn this situation over to God with the knowledge that all I can do right now is love her, no matter what. My worrying won't change her outcome. Self-control means you have learned to bend, because if you're brittle, you'll break."

Ruby MacDonald, who's learned her self-discipline, just like everyone else.

45 YOU'RE COMFORTABLE WITH YOUR BODY

"My body is the most comfortable ever in my life — no more sweaty underarms and elsewhere. No more menstruation."
Doris, age 62.

"I really thought about a face lift. My grandson said 'Why Grandma, if you take away your wrinkles how will we know you're our grandma?' But that wasn't what stopped me. I guess I was part chicken but it came down to I wanted to take a trip with the money instead. I gave up coloring my hair, too. Now it's mousy instead of 'warm brown' but I decided I just didn't need that hassle anymore."
Louise Lothspeich, counselor.

"Do you know anyone who is really satisfied with her face? Though I've never been satisfied with mine, nothing would induce me to change it, or do anything stupid, like lifting it."
Helen Hays, First Lady of American Theater.

"If you have false teeth, you don't have to floss."
Libby Hall, philosopher.

"I'm not so concerned about my looks anymore, because after people get to know me, they look through that to the inner me. [My friend Barbara says you have to make an effort to look good, though, or hope they get to know you really fast]. When you look in older books at pictures of grandmothers, they were nice and round and soft — skinny grandmothers are a relatively recent thing! Maybe it's just a fad that will pass, and I'll be right in fashion."

Alice Musgrove, a wonderful grandmother indeed.

"When you get older, you look better in glasses than you thought you would."

A woman who looks great in her glasses.

46 YOU LEARN TO ENJOY SOLITUDE

"I don't mind being alone, in fact I like it, need it at times. I've always known who I was and felt satisfied with it. I'm very satisfied with me, with my life. I hope that doesn't sound egotistical but I think faith has a lot to do with that. My church is, and always has been, very important to me."
Dot Latting, storyteller and walker.

"I don't mind being alone, in fact, I like it. I can always find something to do, go walking, read, I love to follow the teams in basketball, football, I love sports, still attend some of the home games. I feel sorry for people, women especially who are widowed, who can't stand to be alone. Maybe it comes down to: I like me. I'm good company. And I have no time to be bored."
Hazel Stout, who's been widowed for 15 years.

"If you can't sleep, don't count sheep — talk to the Shepherd. How can I possibly be lonely when I am able to talk to the Shepherd?"
Beatrice Boyd, 92, mother of columnist Malcolm Boyd.

YOU RECOGNIZE AND USE YOUR SKILLS AND TALENTS

"I like to start something, to inaugurate good things. I can look at a need, see a problem and get excited about finding a solution. I get a thrill out of getting it going, finding and training good volunteers, someone to head it up. And I seem to have a knack for finding funding to make it all happen. For example, the literacy program I started through Friends of the Library years ago. Our church's Vietnam family wanted so badly to learn English that it turned into a program for thousands.

"Then when one project is going strong, something else usually comes along and I jump into that one. I know that part of my success is the vast network of people I know and can call on.

"My causes have turned into an eight-hour-a-day job since I retired from teaching in 1971."

Grace Parker, who continues to work with literacy because one in five people in our country is functionally illiterate.

Evelyn Day Colliton could have let her years and broken health keep her from using her skills and talents as an ex-English teacher, but she didn't. She was hired by a local high school to be a lay reader for the English department. She's been correcting papers for 35 years. "People think this is easy," she said, holding up a handful of papers. "But sometimes it takes me an hour or two to correct just one page. Of course, sometimes my corrections are longer than the papers.

"I'm a perfectionist," she says. "Whatever I do, I do to the best of my ability. If I don't know how to do it, I set about learning how. I expect my students to work as hard as I do."

Teachers request her services and the students who get to know her, usually because they won her $1,000 scholarship, praise her skill and thank her for her red penciling.

At 92, Colliton has no plans to retire. There are still students who need her.

A GOOD MARRIAGE GETS BETTER

"I love being alone again with this wonderful man I married 35 years ago. Sharing the memories of all those good times, sad times, trying times. Building new memories to share on our 50th anniversary."
Aris Painter, executive nurse.

"One good thing is that I've learned how to manage George. He manages the motel we're at and I manage him. It works great. Didn't know how to do this for 30 years."
Del Voorhees, manager.

"All those years when we were raising our kids and just trying to keep up, we had so little time for each other. Now we've had the time and we've learned to take the time to be a friend to the person we married. Now we're best friends."
J. and P. Hansen.

"Not long ago," said Ruth Stafford Peale, "my husband, who's 93, was speaking at the 25th anniversary for the pastor who succeeded Norman at Marble Collegiate Church in New York. He held

3,000 people spellbound and roaring with laughter for 16 minutes without a note. At one point he picked up his watch and said, 'I know I was only to talk for seven minutes but I can't see my watch and besides, it isn't running very well. My wife won't let me buy a new one because she says I won't live long enough to wear it out.' "

The Peales, who are a classic example of an abiding marriage, on their way to three weeks in Hong Kong to help at the kindergartens the Peale Foundation has established there.

Jimmy Stewart on his 40-year+ marriage to Gloria McLean: "It's good . . . darn good . . . I guess it's that way because Gloria and I really like each other . . . and we're not afraid to show it."

*From **The Saturday Evening Post**, May-June 1988.*

"My mother had a beautiful life, a husband who adored her, four healthy children, wonderful friends. Yet she would always say, 'When my ship comes in' — daydream about what she would do someday. Well, much as I loved her, I don't believe in that. There ought to be joy in life now, this moment. My ship came in when I married George and raised our children."

*First Lady Barbara Bush, from **Woman's Day**, October 10, 1990.*

"My wife and I usually go out for breakfast on Saturday morning and we're laughing, telling jokes and cutting up and there all those people sit around us with their faces hangin' down in their soup. I just can't figure 'em. The world musta' treated them pretty bad. Glad my life's not like that."

Bob Rheinhart, who is happily married.

"I have a loving wife who loves me despite my deficiencies, which she does tend to point out every once in awhile. While I could be more supportive, she's the cuddler type and watches out for me. She'll say 'The cords of your neck are standing out, what kind of new project are you into now?' We're a real team."

Dr. Lendon H. Smith.

49 YOU LEARN TO APPRECIATE YOUR SPOUSE'S CONTRIBUTIONS

"When I worked away from home at my job, I used to wonder what my wife did all day. I knew she took care of the house and raised our kids, but from the outside, that didn't seem to be so hard. Now that I'm retired I realize how much effort goes into a house. And now the kids aren't even there."
Harvey Kolstad.

"Did you know that you can spend the entire day cooking and cleaning up? That laundry, even for only two people, takes time? Now that I'm retired and share these duties, I realize how much time they take. All these years my wife did it all. I don't know how she managed, besides raising the kids."
A retired plumber.

"All those years my husband went off to his job, even though sometimes he sure didn't feel like it. Well, I know I always appreciated it, but when I went to work outside the home after the kids grew up, then I *really* appreciated him and what he did."
A woman still in the workforce.

YOU'RE GRATEFUL YOU STAYED MARRIED THROUGH THE BAD TIMES

The Jennings' marriage seemed to be on auto-pilot until scandals broke about their extra-marital lives. They took a hard look at what they had and decided their marriage was too important to let come apart. Now Peter Jennings says, "When you've been tested by fire, you discover what is truly meaningful in your life. Humor is meaningful. Respect is meaningful. Love is meaningful. We have all three...we laugh today more than ever."

Peter Jennings at 52, from **Good Housekeeping***, April 1991.*

"I loved the '60s and the '70s when feminism came into being. I became more outspoken and assertive and that was hard for my husband to handle. My job as a reporter and then editor caused problems too, because I was well known in the community. My job took a great deal of time, both daytime and evenings, and was very social. In our small community, everything was directed to me. I was respected and having a wonderful time after all the years spent rearing five children. My husband was unhappy with the entire situation. He didn't care for all the activity and he didn't like being Mr. Phyllis Roth. It was extremely hard for me to leave that when he wanted to retire. There were days when I thought of throwing in the towel, but now I'm glad we didn't. We've worked it all through and have enjoyed our years here in the West."

Phyllis Roth, an activist who raised her daughters to become feminists.

"Infidelity is a hard thing to forgive and forget, but it is possible. Takes time and a lot of hard work, but marriages can be rebuilt and it's worth the effort. We know because we did it. Counselors help, biting your tongue is a good trait to develop, loving in spite of, and remembering why you married that person and all the years you've put in make renewal possible."

Two people who realized that marriage vows, in spite of being broken, are renewable.

A SECOND MARRIAGE CAN BE RICHEST OF ALL

"I met Dave here at the retirement center. It was instant attraction. Talk about compatible, we love doing all the same things, travel, entertaining, reading, just being together. He is such a kind and caring person. We both say our lives might have been even happier if we'd met the first time around. But we're just glad for now."

Helen Bryant, living it up at a life-care facility.

"The financial struggles are behind you, the kind that made your younger marriage more difficult. Now we're more secure. And you don't have worry about having children. We work together on the housework which doesn't happen much when you're young. Now there's time to center on just the two of us."

Cliff and Retha Huffman, enjoying each other.

"Today I am a woman. I'm not a scared little girl anymore. Most women never find this kind of happiness once. I have found it twice. I look out the window at David, now retired from his practice, returning from a solitary hike and I smile. Peace."

June Alyson Ashrowe, happy again with her marriage to David Ashrowe.

"My wife of 49 years died when I was 84. She and I'd been partners in our real estate business and I sold it after she died. Just didn't want to do it anymore, without my partner. I was alone awhile and had been ill when one day a nurse at the hospital said I should call Elmeta. So I did. Took her out to lunch. Now she was a right pretty little lady so we went on from there. And here I am at 91 with a busy wonderful wife, a good mind and on a scale of one to ten, a body at minus 30. It's not doing so good but I've lived a good life. What more can you ask?"

Byron Cavnar, a gallant gentleman.

"In this country, your worth is measured by how much money you make. After two disastrous marriages, I grew to the point that I was making a lot of money myself. Therefore, when I married again, much to my surprise because I swore I was done with marriage, I didn't need to look for security. In fact, I wasn't even really in love, I married a very good friend. And that, for me, has been the best way to go."

Kristen Johnson Ingram, author.

"My wife and I were married for 57 years when she died. I was single for four years when this beautiful, much younger woman came into my life. We married and she is a major reason for my happiness."

Dr. Cecil Osborne, who knows how to recognize happiness and helps others find it.

"After a miserable divorce in my 40s, I stayed in counseling for two and a half years. During that time I not only got to know myself and heal from the divorce, I came away with a much clearer sense of what would be important to me if I should meet another man I wanted to marry.

"You know, when you're young, you go into marriage due to raging hormones. I didn't want to do that again. I liked being single, loved being alone, being in charge of me and managing a successful lifestyle for myself.

"I entered the dating scene with terror. Who knew what the new rules were, how to set boundaries, how to meet the kind of men I might like to be with.

"But through it all I knew I wanted to be valued for who I was and for my gifts and talents. I wanted a man who had a good sense of who he was, was fun to be with, a good sense of humor and wanted to share my life. I didn't need to look for someone to support me financially because I was doing all right.

"I found him or he found me. Norm and I are deeply happy and good for each other."

Sally Stuart, writer, teacher.

52 SEX FREQUENTLY GETS BETTER

"My wife and I've been married 50 years and not too long ago I went to a new doctor for a check-up. She was a Jewish woman, 35, 40. She asked, 'How's your sex life, Mr. Rheinhart?' I looked at her and said, 'Well, not like when I was 25. Had to cut down to twice a night.' "
Bob Rheinhart, happily married.

"There's more freedom for your relationship between husband and wife. You can have sex on the kitchen table if you want — but only if you've changed the locks and shut up the pets."
A candid woman.

"Lovemaking doesn't have to diminish or end at 40, 50, 60 — or any age. On the contrary, think of this as a time to change your approach to sex, rather than give up on it, and you will learn to make your sexual life better than ever."
From the book Sex After 40, by Saul H. Rosenthal, M.D.

"It's not how hard your penis is but how well you

use it (and the rest of your body) that will determine how much you please your partner during lovemaking."

*Saul H. Rosenthal, M.D. in **Sex After 40**.*

"You may have retired from sexual awareness, but you can always go back to work. As with swimming, you never forget the strokes."

*David Brown in **The Rest of Your Life is the Best of Your Life**.*

OR YOU MAY DISCOVER YOU DON'T NEED SEX TO BE HAPPY

"One good thing is that I'm not so driven by sexual needs so I'm more relaxed."

BURIED TREASURE
Lodged below,
Source of pleasure,
Now of woe.
Erstwhile loyal,
Now apostate--
How you foil me
Now, old prostate.
David Goldstein.

"Frankly, I deeply resent the show-biz approach to the private lives each of us has a right to, and having started my adult life feeling guilty about too much sex, I'll be damned if I'll end my days feeling guilty about too little."

*Eda LeShan from her book **It's Better to be Over the Hill Than Under It.***

"The 'no thanks' group has its own factions: those who just don't want to bother anymore; those who had it so good that they don't want to threaten their memories with any new, less satisfying experiences; those who, because of 'engine failure' can't — or think they can't . . . denied that kind of affection [we felt before], we won't risk sex. Some of us fall back on masturbation, the satisfaction we discovered as adolescents. Others simply do without."

*Florence Mason, in **To Love Again.***

54 FOR SOME THERE'S MORE SEXUAL FREEDOM

"I think healthy men and women, regardless of other commitments, evaluate each other as sexual partners when they first meet. Circumstances decide how far the relationship is likely to go. It needn't go too far. I find women don't want to be bedded as much as desired and admired . . . [which is] sometimes enough — and safer."

*David Brown, in his book **The Rest of Your Life is the Best of Your Life**.*

"This is one of the joys of my life. After my husband became incapacitated, I decided on an affair. I love to go dancing and I met a man at one of the local country club dances. When the relationship edged toward sexual, I didn't stop it. It was wonderful to feel romantic feelings again, to feel desired and pursued. The relationship has continued for several years and we are both content with this arrangement — and very discreet. I would hate to cause my husband pain. Sometimes I think he knows and is happy for me for I have the best of both worlds, a caring husband and a romance, too."

Name withheld by request.

YOU SURVIVED PARENTING

"I used to wonder why the good Lord in all His wisdom turned over childbearing to kids who weren't even dry behind the ears yet, why it wouldn't have been better to wait a little longer, let us develop a little sense before we got into it. But I can see now He was pretty smart. If we'd have known more, we would have skipped right over it."
Cliff Huffman, retired railroad man.

"You finally find out if all those years of parenting worked. So much time — love — effort goes into rearing kids and you never know at the time if you are doing it right. Until they're grown. And have kids of their own. Hopefully they'll live close enough so you can see them at least every few weeks."
Aris Painter, executive nurse, mother, wife.

"I'm really happy with my kids. They've turned into good people and now we're able to be friends. There is a special feeling when your kids are your friends. And besides that, they've given us grand-kids who are cute and bright, real achievers too. It's like living with your own kids again but this time they go home."

Del Voorhees, another of those totally non-prejudiced grandparents.

"There are certain advantages in growing older, like learning not to expect too much of your children, no matter what age they are. Some win prizes, some don't. Some get in trouble with the law, some don't. There's not a hell of a lot you can do about it, so why make yourself miserable?"

*From Lucile Bogue's book **I Dare You! How To Stay Young Forever.***

"There's more open communication today between parents and their children. Parents these days are letting their young people know that they know what the score is. I'm not sure my parents knew much about what was going on."

Ruth Stafford Peale, savvy parent.

"You have to love your children unselfishly. That's hard. But it's the only way."

*First Lady Barbara Bush, from **Good Housekeeping**, November 1989.*

56 YOU BECOME FRIENDS WITH YOUR CHILDREN

"It's kind of nice when you live long enough for your children to be retired so you can do all kinds of things together. We travel together, kind of egg each other on. Like the white water rafting I want to do. There's a special sense of closeness when you can go on an adventure with your daughter."
Hazel Stout, sky diver at 88.

"The real blessing of retired life and having the children all grown and on their own, is that now they're adults, I can know them as adults. Not this mother/child relationship. I get to enjoy them as people. I'm available to them if they need me, but now we're friends."
Bewlay Maney, who says she wouldn't trade all the experiences in her life, good or bad.

"At some point, I'm not sure when, my daughters changed from my daughters to equal people. Even after they were grown there was still this element of worry, would they chose the right job, marry the right man. But at some point, I let go. I realized I couldn't take care of them anymore. Now we're friends. My daughter and I were at a concert and it was just like talking to any of my other friends. I'd chose her for a friend, even if she wasn't my daughter."

Ruth Heintz, who has two wonderful daughters.

"I'm proud my sons have become men I can respect. They're fun to be around and they're good citizens, responsible people. Now I can do things with them and not feel I have to be in charge. For a few years there, I wasn't sure this kind of relationship could happen. I always wanted to be able to help my kids with building or remodeling on their houses and that's happening. Working together like that is one of my dreams come true. I just wish our daughter had lived beyond 21 so I could know her and be excited about what she's doing, too. She and I had a real close relationship and I would have loved to see it grow like it has with the boys."

Wayne Snelling, who doesn't always have the words to tell his kids how proud he is of them.

YOU ARE GIVEN GRANDCHILDREN

"The greatest reason to have children is so you can have grandchildren. I didn't get to enjoy my kids, there were always too many problems. I spent 16 years learning to be an engineer but no one taught me how to be a father. One of the most important jobs we have is to be a parent . . . and grandpa."
Dick Cavnar, loving his children and their children.

"Wow! Are they great! Spoil them rotten — give them back — and laugh. Revenge is sweet!"
Aris Painter, executive nurse.

"Since I love to paint, it's been really thrilling to see my granddaughter develop her art skills too. I about busted my buttons when her artwork was chosen over 300 other entrants to have her artwork on the cover of the Kansas City Orchestra program. This gives the two of us something in common with lots to talk about."
Mazie Maxey, artist.

"The greatest thing Bob and I could come up with

were the grandchildren. They range from one and a half to almost nine and we wouldn't take anything for them. We get to do the fun things with them we didn't have time to do with our own kids. And then we give 'em back, after we spoil them."
Bob and Dale Allen.

"I have a shirt that says 'If I'd known grand-children were so much fun, I'd have had them first.' I wear it a lot."
Bob Allen.

"One of the most enjoyable things of growing old is grandchildren. This is a second marriage for both of us and between us we have eight grandchildren. They're fun. We have no responsibility for them, so you can choose to do the fun things, like when my three grandsons wanted to learn to cross stitch. I bought them each a cheap little kit and we stitched. We spoil 'em and send 'em home. The grandkids think the boat Cliff is building is the greatest thing ever. Can't wait to go out on it."
Retha Huffman, a happy grandma.

"I could never understand why people were so batty over their grandchildren until mine came into my life. Everything they do, everything they are is precious. I'm looking forward to watching them grow, watching them become."
Sally Stuart, writer, speaker, teacher.

"Ninety-nine of your 100 good things [that happen as you grow older] are having a granddaughter. She's just a little doll. One friend says she thinks I go to church just to show off my pictures of her.

"I love sharing pictures with others so I have my pictures on circuit. I always include a self-addressed stamped envelope and they return them. It works great, just sometimes people don't return them quick enough."

Kathleen Fuller, a smart new grandmother.

"I've learned to keep my mouth shut. I have no opinions at all when it comes to rearing the grandkids."

A wise grandmother.

"I never had a burning desire to be a grandparent, but now I feel it's one of life's greater pleasures — feeling those loving little hands patting my face."

Grandpa Walter Cronkite.

"It's wonderful to know that someone out there needs me."

John Curtis, nine years a foster grandparent.

"When my son had the temerity to have a child, I hung up a sign in my office, 'The first one to call me Grandpa gets fired.' Not all of us think grandkids are the greatest — but that was before I met mine."

Tony Barrett.

58 YOU EXPERIENCE UNCONDITIONAL LOVE

"Grandchildren, mine range from four to 24, are the cream, par excellence, to be so totally loved. They think you are wonderful, don't even see your warts and wrinkles. And with them I am able to love unconditionally too."

Louise Lothspeich, counselor.

"Having grandchildren was my first experience of unconditional love. I say in one of my books that God is a grandmother because God loves me the same way I love Andy and Adam, Victor, James and little Mack. The love never changes. I think they're wonderful and God thinks I'm wonderful."

Kristen Johnson Ingram, a typically proud grandma.

"I have to admit to the truth, that I didn't always love my children unconditionally. But it's different with the grandkids. That unconditional love goes both ways. I believe God gives us grandchildren so we can undo some of the mistakes we made as parents. I can love them and have the joy they give me without putting all kinds of expectations on them. "

Pat Cavnar, who hugs her grandkids.

59 YOU SEE THE CONTINUITY OF LIFE IN GREAT-GRAND-CHILDREN

"I have seven grandchildren and six great-grandchildren and they've all loved to come and hear the stories I make up about the animals around here.

"Latting, my great-grandson who is five, said to me, 'Dot, let's walk out in the pasture and you can tell me stories about the animals. We need to get away from all these grown-ups so we can talk.' "
Dot Latting, a doting great-grandma.

"You're more free to enjoy your grandchildren and great-grandchildren because you don't have to buy the shoes."
Hazel May Rue.

"I look at my grandchildren and now their children and I see how life continues. While mine is running out, theirs are just beginning. The family will keep on going. Circumstances change and lifestyles change but family is family. Baby hands and faces are the same from generations on. Babies are new life . . . It's a wonder all right."
Daniel Johnson, proud his family.

110

7

YOU UNDERSTAND AND APPRECIATE YOUR PARENTS

"We've had both of our mothers here with us at different times. It's not always easy but I do it because I want to, not because I have to. I want to help return some of the happiness they gave us."

Retha Huffman, who loves counted cross stitch, dachshunds and being married to Cliff.

"When my mother died after ten-plus years in a rest home, I realized that I'm an orphan. My wife's mother died about the same time and since both our fathers died young, it hit us. We're orphans with only our children to look after. While my mother's death was more a blessing, I realized that I can't even remember the last time I had nurturing parents. So when you are awarded the honor of Patriarch by death, even though you've been acting in that capacity for years, there is now a kind of lonesomeness. Whether your mother was well or not, she was still there, still your mother and now that is no more. But you know you did what had to be done and you got through it. There's good in that."

Weatherman and son Jim Bosley.

"I come from a long living family, grandparents, parents, in their 90s and beyond. Grandmother was always looking for new recipes, she cooked until in her 90s, that's the kind of thing that keeps a person young at heart."

Kathleen Fuller, who has a lot of living left to do.

The Bush family was celebrating George's mother's 88th birthday. George asked his mother, "Tell me, Mom, about your best birthday."

Dorothy Bush, now very frail, reached for her son's hand and said, "I think this one is the best. My son is President of the United States."

*From an article about Barbara Bush in **Good Housekeeping**, November 1989.*

"A highlight was my trip back to the family homestead. Having my 95-year-old mother bake my 80th birthday cake and do most of the cooking for the shindig — well, I have a lot to live up to."

Oliver Graham, who's enjoying a super busy retirement.

"My father and I had a 'touchy' relationship for 30 years after my mother died. For a month before he died, I spent many, many hours beside his bed in the hospital and then the nursing home. You know, we worked it out, somehow. I'm so pleased we had that time together and became so close."

P.B., whose father will be with her all her years.

YOU HAVE INCREASING INTEREST AND PRIDE IN YOUR HERITAGE

"I grew up in British Columbia, daughter of an extremely traditional Chinese family. We were taught to be quiet, not question. Besides that, I was very shy because I knew I was different and therefore not as good as the other children. At school, the children thought I was stuck up but that was not the case at all.

"Now I know or have learned that I am outgoing, a good speaker, I like being around other people. My entire life has been helping others achieve healing in the whole person. Not separate body and mind like doctors treat their patients here.

"I'm grateful for my Chinese background because I can draw on the centuries of medical knowledge that has been passed down in my family; things like the use of herbs, acupuncture, ti chi, understanding the qi (pronounced chee) which means the essence of life. I combine that with my western medical training as a nurse and other schooling and thus bring the best of both worlds together in a way that truly brings healing to my patients."

Dr. Effie Chow, founder of The East/West Center for the Healing Arts.

"I live at Mount Airy, a plantation in Tennessee that is listed in the National Historic Register. Seven generations have lived here. This is the home place where my three very interesting children, their wonderful children and my great-grandchildren are always welcome. We've kept traditions alive here, like during the holidays. As many as can, come home, all ages. What a time we have."

Dot Latting, DAR member.

"You find yourself wanting to know more about your past, your ancestors, what happened when, so you can pass that heritage on to your grandchildren and great-grandchildren."

Pat Rushford.

"I'm not sure who gave whom the gift when I met my Great Aunt Teckla for the one and only time. I was mesmerized by her tale of coming to this country via clippership from Poland. They were caught in a calm with provisions going low. Then their captain refused to take on survivors from a sinking ship for fear his own would not make it. When they reached New York, the children were forced to steal to survive.

"All my life I've been grateful she took the time to tell me her piece of family history."

Leonard Tworek, who is proud of his Polish heritage.

62 YOU APPRECIATE FAMILY TRADITIONS AND HOLIDAYS

"Christmas is one of my favorite times of the year because that's when my family gets together. I love it when my eldest daughter writes our family Christmas letter, then I send out over a hundred. All the cards and letters pour in, so good to hear from people everywhere, even this once a year.

"There's always so much to do but the Christmas tree is always the loveliest ever, each ornament special and bringing back memories. The waxed stars one daughter made in Brownies, the painted wooden sleigh my sister made, the soldier out of clothespin from a grandson, the wooden spoon with a dried bouquet from my granddaughter who died of cancer at 21.

"Each person, each gift, each twinkling light, special and bringing anew that Jesus is the reason for the season. I love Christmas."

Thelma Sommerseth, who loves traditions and her family.

"Birthdays were always important in our home. When I was a child, we always had homemade ice cream, but with my children, I bought the ice cream. I celebrate mine, too, especially my 85th. We had a most wonderful party with all the family at the Coco Palms.

"A big tradition for me, since I'm Portugese, is the Holy Ghost feast which is held some weeks after Easter. Each church here on the island used to have its own celebration, but now we combine them. Each of the ladies who remembers how, bakes sweet bread, and that and roast beef is distributed to everyone. There's a parade and all kinds of fun things. Now there's an auction and bingo — we really enjoy ourselves.

"In the olden days there was always a dance and many of the young girls found their husbands there. I didn't find my husband there — but mine is a long story!"

Mary Ferreira, who loves a celebration.

"I love holidays and celebrations. Every holiday we have family and friends here. I wouldn't think of not having them. That's part of my life — family and friends and having a good time."

Jackie George, who learned to celebrate from her mother.

63 YOU HAVE CLOSE RELATIONSHIPS WITH FRIENDS

"Now is the time for my friends. Time for dinner, in or out, a movie, visits that I promised my friends but never found time for. Superbowl Sunday found a bunch of men around the TV and the women in the kitchen gabbing. Very chauvinistic set-up but we're mature enough not to give a rip."
Aris Painter, executive nurse.

"As you grow older you need a wide circle of friends so that as some die, you still have others left."
Gloria Chisholm, writer.

"We've moved a lot in our 38 years of marriage and I always worried that it would be hard for our kids. But they made friends right away and so did we. You have to be a good friend in order to have friends. We find ourselves keeping in contact with folks all over Minnesota and even Nebraska."
Del Voorhees, 57, mother, wife and motel manager.

"My husband and I were inseparable, we did

everything together. I often thought that if he died before me, I wouldn't even want to keep on living. I wouldn't be able to. That I would just wish I was dead, too. But my husband died and a friend of ours stepped in to help me. He got me going on things, like fishing, clamming, crabbing; got my mind off death and being alone. We traveled across the country. He got me through a very bad time. He turned my life around, and now I'm an adventurer."
Hazel Stout, 88, grateful to a friend.

"Friends are almost more important than family. I hate to ask my family for help but with my friends, it's okay. There's a group of us, we talk on the phone nearly everyday, check up on each other. If I have to confide in someone, I talk with one special friend."
Flora Euller, 92 and happy with her life.

"I'm finding friends are more important than they used to be. We moved around for years and I keep in contact with many of those people we met. Military life is like that, moving a lot. I use the phone the most because even though I do a lot of writing, I don't like to write letters. Besides, with a phone call, you get in a real visit. Phones are a wonderful invention."
Louise M. Reh, who knows how to be a friend.

"I'm fortunate in that I have good friends, people

that like me and I think they're smart and if they're smart and like me, I must be okay."
Dr. Lendon H. Smith, who's enjoying his retirement.

"You are fortunate if you have more than one friend. You got through this life with a tremendous number of acquaintances, associates, people you have fun with. But having a friend is a very unique situation."
Tony Barrett.

"I find myself becoming aware of the importance of family and friends. They are the most important in life, more than wealth or any kind of success. If I don't have a good relationship with my family and friends to rely on, the rest of it will be kind of empty anyway."
Pat Cavnar, 54, who is enjoying her husband's retirement.

YOU HAVE A GREATER APPRECIATION OF NATURE

"Sitting by a stream — just watching the water splash over a rock. Or following a leaf on its voyage. Seriously studying the cloud formations and putting an anemometer on the roof so you can measure the wind gusts. Sure didn't have time for this 20 years ago."

Aris Painter, executive nurse and budding writer.

"While I'm not into native American things, I do have a spiritual connection to the out-of-doors. We take a trip to Mount Rainier every year and it's like going to Mecca. It's something I just have to do. In active imagination and visualization we call it going to your safe place, a place of incredible affirmations and reassurance. We all need to find where those places are for ourselves."

Louise Lothspeich, counselor.

"My love of birds and all things living led me into a new adventure. My son Tom and I were having lunch in town one day and I said, 'Let's go over and look at the new Saturn dealership that just opened up.' I fell in love with a beautiful blue sport's coupe.

120

Tom said I should look at a four-door but I didn't want an old lady's car. When I asked the salesman to show me the trunk, I was sold. You see, the trunk lip was lower than that on most cars so I can lift my 50-pound sacks of bird seed out easily. By the time you get to be 76, you have to try to make some things easier on yourself.

"Well, a couple of weeks later, someone called to ask how I liked my car. Fine I said. Another person called and asked why I bought that particular car. I told him — I had to get my bird seed out of the trunk. I keep 13 large feeders full all the time. Then an ad agency called from San Francisco asking me to be in an ad for Saturn. I tried to tell them no but the more they talked the more fun it sounded. So I did.

"Three days it took. They wanted to use a tree in my yard but couldn't disguise the light pole. So they moved bird feeders and bird houses down by a huge tree down the road aways. The people were just wonderful. One man, who looked like a real-life Santa Claus with his white hair and beard, said the clothes I laid out wouldn't do. He headed for my closet. I had stashed all my projects in there to get them out of the way, so it all nearly fell on him. A real Fibber McGee joke. I felt like crawling under the bed.

"But I've now been on television, radio, written up in newspapers and magazines. My grandson said the ad would be in *Rolling Stones*, whatever that is.

Let me tell you, shocked wasn't the word when I saw the ad and read some of the magazine, four-letter words . . . my. All of it's been fun."

Velma Willarson, nature lover from a country spot.

"Why not plant a tree in memory of a loved one rather than a tombstone? Trees are powerful beings that help Earth move her life cycles in many different ways — that remind us how Death rebirthes into Life. For now it is enough to know that my simple action (of planting trees) will bring life and beauty to Earth for many, many years to come."

*Patricia Nell Warren, from an article in **Modern Maturity**.*

"Growing things have always fascinated me, so I went back to school after I turned 50 and took some botany classes. Everywhere we go I try to identify the flora and fauna of the area. I feel closer to my new home when I know what grows native there. Now I'm compiling a survey of the trees in my area."

Louise M. Reh, who makes friends with trees.

65 YOU EXERCISE YOUR CREATIVITY

A group of older citizens formed a theater group to entertain without charge at hospitals, nursing homes and senior centers.

"I like the idea of performing," said Allie Patch. "I said to myself, 'Fifty years ago you thought you'd like to do it. Well, go do it now.' "

Mary Bacher said she'd vegetated for six and a half years after her husband died. "Now I feel I'm a productive person, contributing to other's enjoyment and my own. I'm 63 going on 16. If you're going to dream, you might as well dream big."

Lil Granfors used to be a singer but stopped after marriage. Now she sings *That's Life* because it's true. "I had to prove to both myself and my family that I wouldn't embarrass them. Just do your own thing, no matter what." She wants to take up tap dancing next.

Ted Fuller plays the umpire in *Casey at the Bat*. "It's a nice adrenalin rush when you're up on stage. Adrenalin is good for you."

"We all laugh a lot," says John Richards who has done some little theater through the years. "All the time there's never been a harsh word or bad feelings. We all need that. Plus the applause."

Research conducted by gerontologist Lydia Bronte has shown that performance and creativity don't have to diminish with age, particularly if men and women take care of themselves physically.

"I always knew I loved music but now I play backup guitar for old-time fiddlers. I like people and I like music and this way I get more of both. Playing guitar gives me a sense of accomplishment and I just love the sound of guitar and fiddle music. When we play for nursing homes, I get a feeling of appreciation and everyone needs to feel appreciated."
Bob Huffman, who "jams" with other musicians.

"As soon as I hear the music, I forget about my arthritis and my walker. I dance with a troupe which performs in schools, nursing homes and hospitals around Washington, D.C. My weekly schedule includes easy exercise classes at my apartment building, troupe rehearsal and as many as three 50-minute performances. At 94 I show the children they don't have to worry about old age."
*Thelma Tulane, from USA **Weekend.***

"I've always known I was a poet and could get a melody in my head to go with the words but now the part of the gift I think is even more valuable, is that even though I will never write *great* music, I will never move people's souls that way, but I can write music that amateurs can play and do it with enjoyment. I'll never be in music history books, not even as a footnote, but everything I've written is still selling. People who buy these scores are people who play them. They don't just buy them and put them on the shelf."

Dr. David Goldstein, composer.

"When I was about to retire, I asked for paints and supplies as my parting gift from the company I worked for. I attended adult school and private teachers until I decided on acrylics as my favorite medium. I love to paint buildings, mostly from pictures, about 16x20, and those sell well. My husband takes the pictures, all different angles and then I come home, sit down and paint away. He took photography classes at the same time I took painting classes. Our art association has several places to hang our work, like banks, public buildings, churches and a hospital. Painting is my escape instead of TV or reading so I consider the pleasure and relaxation I get in the amount I charge."

Mazie Maxey, artist.

"All the years the children were growing up, I was totally involved, the first-aid station, the water boy for the Cub Scouts. When my girls came along, I started a children's theater group. I was always there for them all.

"I had always enjoyed crafts but never had time for them, so when I retired, I leaped right in. Now I teach smocking as an old-time skill at a local Historical Society Museum. They have a great program there, trying to interest people in a lot of the old-time skills and crafts, from bobbin lace to quilting, tatting to stitchery. It keeps me busy and happy."

Bewlay Maney, who loves her life.

"Two projects I'm mulling over right now. One: I want to go back to all the places of my childhood and photograph them to show what can happen in a life time. It'll take an increase in my skills because I want to do it in black and white. I find the solitary life of a photographer a release, creative. I've done this documentary-still thing before with a multi-media slide show on the waterfront which was well received.

"The second is to write our family history, my thoughts and feelings, to leave for my children, all the stuff that's up in my head. I want to do this before I start to lose contact, before I can't remember anymore. I should have done this with my mother years ago."

Ruth Heintz, who sees through an artist's eyes.

YOU FIND GREAT PLEASURE IN CONTINUING TO LEARN

"When I turned 65 I got a computer. I needed it for writing. Wasn't scary at all. It was just a glorified typewriter."
Louise M. Reh, an adventurer.

"The last couple of years I've learned to ice fish. You know that's a major winter sport here in Minnesota. We always had a fish house but I thought that was a stupid sport. Until I tried it and caught bigger fish than George. It's kind of fun — you get your cribbage board out and if a fish comes along, that's great. Oh, and I've learned to golf too. I didn't have time or money before, but now what the heck. I was a golf widow for too many years and I'm not going to do that anymore. Now we do things together."
Del Voorhees, new sports devotee.

"About three years ago I made a choice between becoming computer literate and relearning the cello which I'd played as a kid. Between cello lessons and my wife and I getting interested in opera, now we buy videos of operas to watch when we want, we've been lifted spiritually, in ways we never imagined. We go to plays and concerts, museums, travel, all the things we never had time to do with our three children and my career. We love cruises.

"I'm taking classes in Western Civilization to make up for my lack. I felt I got gypped out of a liberal arts education because I went into medicine and now I get to make up for that. It's never to late to learn new things, get an education."

Herbert Schwartz, a college professor going back to college.

"My going back to college was for a career change. I had a fine arts degree and used that in interior design but decided I'd like to be involved helping other people with career changes. I went to school nights and it took four years to get my masters in career counseling. The studying and learning wasn't so hard as just getting adjusted to the school atmosphere, figuring out what the teachers wanted. Most of the students were many years younger than I, but that didn't bother me.

"The position I have now uses all my education, intuition and management skills. There's never a dull moment and that's the way I like life."

Betty Zarn, who's making a difference with her second education.

67 YOU DEVELOP A HEIGHTENED SENSE OF ADVENTURE

"One of the high points of my career — at age 50 I was Henry Higgins in *My Fair Lady*. I couldn't remember all the lines but the audience knew them so it was all right. The leading lady was opera material, she had such a lovely voice, and one night she leaned over and said to me, 'Smith, you sing better than Rex Harrison.' Now let me tell you, I was really delighted. I came home and told my wife and she said, 'Len, anybody sings better than Rex Harrison.' "

Dr. Lendon H. Smith.

"My husband was very protective and while we very happy, I never did much outside our home. I raised the family, managed the house and a building we owned but that was about it. After he died, a friend of ours must have detected a tiny flicker of the spirit of adventure in me, so he taught me all kinds of things. We went fishing, ice fishing in Michigan, snowmobiling, scuba diving, floating in a glider over Hawaii, doing things outdoors and all over the country.

"But the highlight is thanks to my daughter. Her

husband sky-dives and she thought jumping out of an airplane would be a good way for me to celebrate my 88th birthday. I was a bit scared when we were up in the plane, but once we were hooked together in some kind of contraption and stepped out on that platform — well, I'd do it again. We just stepped off into air — nothing. We free-fell for about a mile, then the chute opened and I was in awe as the valley around Fresno came slowly up to meet me. I kept my eyes open the entire time, didn't want to miss a minute. All the colors and the quiet, the sense of freedom. I was a bird for those minutes.

"I think I'll go white water rafting on the Colorado this next summer. There should be some thrills there too."

Hazel Stout, 88, who'll try almost anything.

For the 12th time, Audrey Sutherland paddled her own inflatable canoe along Alaska's inland passage. She's logged 7,000 miles in 23 years. "Sometimes you have to do the important things and not wait to say, 'I wish I had . . .' "

Audry Sutherland, only older chronologically.

"Well, you see, I was just sitting there telling him [Dustin Hoffman during the filming of *Rain Man*] some stories about the early days of Oklahoma, like when they stole the state seal from Guthrey and took it to Oklahoma City and then issued a proclamation that Oklahoma City was now the state capitol. Told him about the Pony Express too. They were filming away but I was just having a great time talking with him. He didn't answer me anything though, just kept fiddling with that camera.

"Then this lady came up to me and said they were planning to use what they'd filmed in the movie so would I go down and get signed up for the Screen Actors Guild and they'd pay me $348. Every now and then I get a royalty check in the mail, all told about $3,000 now. How about that?"

"I'm not just interested in history, I'm part of it. Born in 1901 while this was still Indian Territory."

Byron Cavnar, a late-blooming film star.

1. Y

YOU CAN BEGIN EXCITING NEW CAREERS AFTER 50

"Life's been good to me and now it's time to put back," Ethel Levitt told Harry Reasoner on *60 Minutes*. Sometimes referred to as "law mommas," Ethel Levitt, 81, and Grace Quinn, 75, found a place that needed them and went to work. They serve low income clients, those who can't afford high priced legal services and make too much for public assistance.

After their husbands died, they went back to law school and now work full-time without salary. "We work because we're needed," says Levitt.

"I will never lose my interest in early man. I am consumed by a need to know what he ate, how he lived, played and worshiped."

Robert O. Coleman switched from chemist to professor of Hebrew and archaeology. His family thought he was crazy to go back to school at his age. Now he concentrates on his first love, archaeology.

"I know what pot smells like, I give advice on boyfriend trouble, I'll take in a tuck in a dress if needed.

I'm a sorority housemother at Kappa Alpha Theta, UCLA. I do whatever is needed, even at 90. For this job you need experience. You need wisdom. And you need quite a lot of energy. I love it all."

*Ruby Long, from USA **Weekend.***

"I'm leaving my life in a ministry and as an agent for writers, both because it's driving me crazy and because I'm coming nearer to retirement with no pension, no retirement benefits. But I get to stay in the world of books because I'll be working in a library. I'm looking forward to a low-pressure job. I've learned I don't need all the pressure of deadlines and power lunches and rushing around to prove how important I am. I am me and because I am, I am valuable."

Louise Gibbons, retiring literary agent, aspiring librarian.

"As you get older, you learn to work smarter so in a new career you're more successful more quickly. You've learned to eliminate some of the ridiculous stuff you did when you were younger. You learn to be honest and tell people everything up front. You become a better judge of people, able to weed out the time-takers and users. It makes your life easier and more successful."

Marlys Gilbert, who in her 60s is on the fast track to upper management in Mary Kay.

Evelyn Bedell found that a retirement life in Arizona didn't fit.

"One day I heard what I think was God's voice saying, 'Now will you consider going into the ministry?' At first I said no but then I changed my mind and headed for California and three years of seminary. My call was to a small town which again raised some doubts but I fell in love with the people. I work with the elderly and try to fill the gap for those who are able to be active and those in nursing homes. I believe the church is uniquely capable of helping keep older people in their homes longer. I find it good here, there's no place I'd rather be."

*The Reverend Evelyn, who's busy baptizing, marrying, burying and counseling one and all in a small town in Missouri at age 75. From the **AARP Bulletin.***

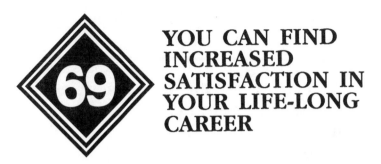

YOU CAN FIND INCREASED SATISFACTION IN YOUR LIFE-LONG CAREER

"I'm content with my life, with the things I've done. It used to be, 'Here I am 45 or 50 and I'm not vice president yet.' That's bad. I'm still not, but I couldn't care less. Now I'm interested in my goals, not what I perceived other people expected of me. While I'm probably harder on myself than anyone, now I'm trying to satisfy me. I appreciate quality, in people, and in things."

Phil Oestricher, pilot/engineer.

"Not a day went by that my career in taking care of sick and dying children didn't remind me to be grateful for the good health of me and my family. Now children that would have died are five-year and longer survivors. That and the teaching has been wonderfully rewarding."

Herbert Schwartz, doctor and father.

"I knew from the time I was knee-high to a grasshopper that I would be a farmer. I knew full well that farming was no easy street but a challenge working with Mother Nature who was capricious but also benevolent, much in concert with human nature.

"Farming gave me a deep sense of walking hand in hand with God — the sky, sun, stars and liquid dew of rain, cloaking us with a closeness seldom found elsewhere. It is like the dawn that wakes up the sleepy night and opens the bright eye of sunlight for the day."

Leonard Tworek, farmer poet.

"If you love your work, you can expand on it at any time in your life. I love my work so work makes my life enjoyable. I enjoy seeing people get better. I see that the meaning of life, as God created us, is to grow and learn. You see this in every blade of grass, every giant Sequoia, this drive to be better. As I work with people and they get better, I'm part of this process. That's the highest enjoyment.

"Right out of the seminary when the depression broke, I gathered a group of 50 people, found a building and put them to work gathering and repairing goods. We fed and housed them. At the same time, I was pastoring a local church.

"While pastoring another church, I founded and organized nine new churches. Then while still a minister, I founded Yokefellows.

"Having challenges all the time energizes me. I thrive on problem-solving. They're fun, I enjoy them. I've enjoyed everything I've done. Somewhere in there I wrote 14 books too. What fun!"

Dr. Cecil Osborne, who has so much fun he forgets he's working.

70 YOU GET SPECIAL PLEASURE OUT OF SHARING YOUR KNOWLEDGE

Rosalie Sadenwater put aside her dreamed of art career to be a wife and mother. Since she held a job besides, she never had time for her own art work.

"At the age of 50 I quit my job and began taking classes at the American Academy of Art in Chicago. It took me five years to get an associate's degree in fine art but through that time I discovered that I'd like to teach besides my own painting. I'd never intended to teach, just thought I'd retire and paint for myself."

She started teaching children but now she teaches ten-week courses for older adults. She especially loves watercolor because there are so many interesting concepts to it. Rosalie realizes not everyone can be a painter but "anyone can learn to draw."

"Introduction of art into someone's life is a nonending learning experience, especially for older people. Drawing is worth all the agony of the learning."

She says that teaching is a whip that keeps both her and her students going. Her education has proved to be educating for plenty of others and it keeps on going.

R.S., who helps other develop.

They teach French or folk dancing or basic computer skills. And their lessons are lapped up by students who enjoy learning from older people. The lessons are part of a *Community in the Schools* program which brings people with special skills in contact with students who need or want them.

"Participating in this program gives me satisfaction and it helps the school system and the kids," says one former teacher who's now teaching for fun.

"I like writing a whole lot better," said one student after working with a visiting writer. "And the volunteers don't treat us like kids."

You could help make it happen in your community.

David Lee is a landscaper by trade and his job is maintaining the grounds of a private grade school. But when the kids are out for recess or lunch, he entertains them with tales of his boyhood on a Louisiana sharecropper's farm. He tells them what it was like growing up black in the South before integration, what it was like being dirt-poor and always owing the landowner, what it was like knowing your daddy loved you so much he'd give you part of his supper. David Lee has learned to laugh and sing in spite of what happens, and he shares that with the children too.

Lee has taped his stories, and like stories from countless other people, his tapes have become part of the living history in a local historical society.

*From the **Contra Costa Times**, 1986.*

71 YOU HAVE A NEW APPRECIATION OF OLD SAYINGS

"What you've done in the past comes home to roost. I see this more and more."
Patricia Pratico who runs a playhouse for community theater.

" 'Don't let the sun go down on your anger.' Hard to live up to, but good for building character. I said it plenty of times to my children, too."
Audrey Miller, with wise advice from an old saying.

"My mother used to say, 'Never say never,' and I know now that it's easier to live life without absolutes and ultimatums. She also used to say, 'Be careful, or you might get what you wish for.' Now occasionally when I have, it's been a mistake!"
P.B., more careful now about her wishes.

"I heard someone quote a verse about reaping ten times what you sow. To me that means that what you give out, you get back ten times over. That makes me real careful about what kind of stuff I put out there. Say you ream someone out, who needs that back ten times? But if you give hugs, I'll take my ten times back gladly."

L.S., a lover of truisms, old sayings, words to live by.

"The ones that used to keep children in line are still good:

> Little pitchers have big ears.
> Children should be seen and not heard.
> If wishes were horses, beggars would ride.
> Money doesn't grow on trees.
> Idle hands are the devil's workshop.

And just in case a child thought a bit highly of himself:

> Handsome is as handsome does.
> Beauty is only skin deep.

I say them to my grandchildren!"

Arlene Pike, whose grandchildren love her.

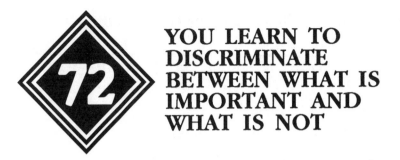

YOU LEARN TO DISCRIMINATE BETWEEN WHAT IS IMPORTANT AND WHAT IS NOT

"As I've gotten older, I've come to realize I don't have the boundless energy I had when younger. That forces me to focus on the important things which means I've learned to recognize the difference. Doesn't mean I always do it but I'm getting better at making good choices."

Sarah Jones, who tries to discriminate between important and not-so and down-right trivial.

"When I was raising my kids, I thought clothes that matched, preferably clean and patched, was important. Now I'm just grateful when my children and grandchildren stay clean and sober, meaning no drugs or alcohol. My definition of important has really changed."

Barbara Rader, who has been through many changes.

"When we were first married, we'd fight over the most trivial things, like socks on the floor, hair in the sink, coming home a few minutes late. Now I wish I had all the energy I wasted on that stuff. You could say we're more laid back, but I think we've given up on the little things or changed them when necessary. But it goes beyond that. The important things are loving each other, being kind and gentle, finding good things to say rather than nag. It works — we've been married 45 years."

A happy couple working toward their 50th.

"Family, friends, love are the really important things. Everything else is just window dressing. But I didn't know that when I was young."

A grammy who cares.

YOU REAP THE REWARDS OF GOOD FINANCIAL PLANNING

> The over-50 group already controls 70 percent of the nation's financial assets and 50 percent of the discretionary income.

"I grew up in the depression and saving was always pounded into you. We had savings books in grammar school and would bring in a penny a day or a nickel a week. Therefore my wife and I made it a habit to save ten percent of our earnings and now I'm in the good-news position that my annuities are paying me about 80 percent of my former income. I see this as the reward for saving. I wasn't a big investor, but a saver. Somewhere I picked up the message, 'You're only as good as the money you save.' It sounds very old-fashioned but I'm an example that it works."

Herbert Schwartz, retired M.D.

"I can now afford a cleaning lady. I never could before."

Alice Musgrove, who has better things to do.

"It's interesting. While I have less money coming in now than when I was working, I have more spendable money — money that can buy things I want. I have most of the things I need."
Oliver Graham.

"Retirement hasn't brought all the things I dreamed because my legs and heart are bad, but then I don't have any financial worries either. We have all the necessities and the house is paid for, for which I'm grateful."
"Bing" Bingham, a retired military officer.

"We're the group who lived through the Great Depression so I think we look at financial things a bit differently. We don't fear poverty, we know you can live through it. We never felt poor then, we just learned to exchange and share. Everyone was in the same boat. When the chips were down, we came through — for ourselves and for each other."
From some people who learned how to cope.

"Because of the depression, I resolved to never get caught in that circumstance again. Therefore, I've always been careful with my money. I know saving for a rainy day is laughed at now, but I'm financially secure because I believed it."
A wise and careful man.

YOU ARE ELEGIBLE FOR AGE-RELATED DISCOUNTS

"At first I was embarrassed to speak up for discounts at restaurants, travel places, department stores. Now I figure, hey, why not? Makes my money stretch farther."

A man no longer too proud for a good deal.

"We watch for places that offer senior discounts and take advantage of them. Why not? We earned it."

Pat Tweitmoe.

"I've seen plenty of the country thanks to discounts on buses, planes and my favorite, the train. I love when you can buy a ticket that lets you go anywhere within a certain time period. New England is unbelievable in the fall, Florida feels good in the winter and spring in the Rockies is a sight to behold. I'll keep on traveling as long as I'm able."

Mabel Highnes, who takes advantage of discounts to feed her wanderlust.

YOU BENEFIT FROM ALL THOSE YEARS YOU PAID INTO SOCIAL SECURITY

"I know we all belly-ached about the Social Security [funds] taken out of our paychecks, but now that it comes back every month in the form of a check, I'm grateful. It isn't easy all the time, living on a fixed income, but without my SS check, I wouldn't make it."

John Barnes, a retired auto worker.

"I manage my money better now and I have the security of a pension and Social Security. I'm more affluent now, I'm comfortable. I already have all the necessities, so I needn't spend money there, and I'm no longer saving for a rainy day or for when I'm old. Now I *am* old, so I spend it."

Bob Huffman, who is really living his retirement.

"I have never been anything but a housewife, so though my husband died before he collected anything, I was able to get his Social Security. I also received his insurance but the company said I wouldn't be eligible for his pension. Six years later they told me I could claim a small pension — $14!

"Now I'm living in HUD housing and since I earn

only a bit over $600 in Social Security, that is what makes it possible for me to live on my own. My daughters would take me in I know, I have wonderful daughters, but I like living here on the islands where I've always lived. Without Social Security I couldn't live this way, so I am happy."

Mary Ferreira, who loves her home.

"If I didn't have Social Security from my husband, the only income I would have would be what I can make babysitting. That's one reason I live here in a small town in North Dakota. Besides having relatives here, there is nowhere else I could live cheaper. That Social Security check is what keeps me independent."

Clara Rasmussen, one of the many widows in this country who lives on Social Security.

76 MEDICARE IS A MAJOR HELP WITH MEDICAL BILLS

"I have had no trouble with Medicare; it helps me live on the amount I have. I am diabetic so I see the doctor fairly often, but I never even have to worry about the paperwork. I get copies to show it is all taken care of. I have extra insurance that I pay quarterly and I pay a small fee for each doctor's visit but that is all. Any hospital visits are covered the same way. I get good care, so I am happy. How else would I pay for all the things I need?

Mary Ferreira, who appreciates the system.

"When my husband was alive and in and out of the hospital and nursing home so often, we couldn't have managed without Medicare. Our home, our savings, everything would have been eaten up and then some. I know some people complain about the paperwork and that sometimes things get messed up, but I am so grateful for the way our medical bills were taken care of. We carry Blue Cross too, and I have to pay for that, but I don't mind. For us it all worked like it should."

Thelma Sommerseth, who didn't hesitate to have cataract surgery, thanks to Medicare.

"I had a five-place by-pass surgery three years ago. I know the bills totalled around $50,000. How would we have ever paid something like that without Medicare? We'd have been in hock to the hospitals for the rest of our lives, or else they would never have done the surgery, and then I wouldn't be here at all. Think if we'd have had to sell our house to pay the medical costs. I know there is a lot of controversy about Medicare, but we're sure grateful for the coverage."

Harriett Glandon, a living example of the benefits of Medicare.

YOU DISCOVER YOUR HARD-EARNED SKILLS ARE STILL MARKETABLE

Days Inn Hotel chain offers job fairs for seniors because they've found older employers more responsible, learn quicker, show up for work on time and understand the idea of customer service.

"Only older workers need apply," declared Texas boat builder, Al Brooks. "It's time to coin a new term — multi-skilled, experienced workers. Younger people may have one skill but an older fellow can install Formica, do framing, finishing and a lot of other jobs. They take something different and figure it out."

Al Brooks hired four mature non-boat-builder crafts-people with one experienced boat builder to custom-build a high-tech, 57-foot-sailing yacht. They'll serve as team leaders of future projects, this one went so well.

"Don't retire . . . age is just a number. I'm really against seniors retiring. We have seniors working in our restaurants . . . who are 80 years old. They're fantastic. They enjoy it. They know all the customers. People who have always been busy need to be busy."

Dave Thomas, founder of Wendy's, in his book **Dave's Way.**

"When you get to be my age, the idea is to get the job done with as little work as possible."

George Burns, 95, from his book **Wisdom of the Nineties.** *It may be an understatement to say that his skills are still marketable!*

"Life for me is an adventure. If I stay too long in one job, I loose sight of the possible adventures around me — and I stagnate. I can't let that happen, but now as I'm older and jobs are more scarce and I'm in a secure job, it's harder to let it go. But I will do so because my skills are versatile, as I am."

Pauline Goodrich, who's zest for living is exciting to be around.

YOU FIND NEW EXCITEMENT IN STARTING YOUR OWN BUSINESS AFTER 50

"I'd been a high school counselor ever since college when one day a colleague said he was opening a private practice and there was an extra office in the space. He suggested I take it. I went home, thought about it overnight, turned in my resignation at the school and a few days later, I was in business. I've always believed that when a door opens, you should go through. All manner of exciting things wait on the other side."

Louise Lothspeich, counselor.

"I retired on a Friday, went to church on Sunday and had my first job in yard maintenance on Monday morning. My retirement was one day. I love getting up now — working for myself makes all the difference. Now it's one day at a time."

Bob Allen, landscape and yard maintanence.

"Two things got me thinking after I retired from the second company I started. I was playing golf with a lot of people older than I was, I was 58, and they kept saying they didn't have enough to do and if they did have, they didn't have enough money to do it with. Then I saw a television ad put out by the National Council on Aging. It showed an empty rocker in motion on an empty stage and a voice said, 'Get off your rocker.' So I did.

"I started Retiree Skills, Inc. here in Tucson. We're a temporary employment organization that only uses seniors. There's a tremendous talent pool out there just going to waste if employers would only realize it. Our company helps them do that."

Bob Rheinhart, founder of Retiree Skills, Inc.

"We kind of stumbled into our business. Our daughter went away to school and wrote back so homesick, so I sewed her a lamb and enclosed a card with a message about hugs. Soon I was sewing them for her friends and now we send several styles and sizes of lambs and lamb greeting cards all over the country. Each year our greeting card line expands as I come up with new ideas. We have them for all occasions, and now a Christmas selection too. I've hired people for sewing, but the cards I design myself. Running a business out of your home brings new challenges, but Bob and I can work on this together. Besides, you should read the responses we get from satisfied customers. Our wool lambs truly are a message of love."

Jean and Bob Lamb, who are still excited about their business.

x

79 YOU'VE LIVED LONG ENOUGH TO GET RECOGNITION

"I was honored to be chosen 'Nurse Executive of the Year' for the Oregon Organization of Nurse Executives. It was the first year for the award (1989) and a total surprise. What a wonderful event."
Aris Painter, nurse executive.

"Here I am, 95 years old, and I like what I'm doing. I like getting out of bed to be interviewed. If I was making felt hats, you wouldn't be sitting here."
*George Burns, in his book **Wisdom of the Nineties.***

"In '87 I was awarded Alumni of the Year from Eastern Montana College of Education and I had to get testimonies from everyone [former students] about my teaching. I think I'm the only one who had one from a penitentiary. But my fan had learned to read and he's never forgotten me."
Hazel May Rue, who volunteered to teach the 3 R's in a prison.

"You never know what good things you do in life

154

will come back around. When I taught drama in Manila I had a student who was painfully shy. I kept encouraging her — she had a nice singing voice — and after she left me, she went to London to drama and voice school. Not too long ago I received a letter from her with a ticket inside. She is now starring in *Miss Saigon* on Broadway. And wants me to come see her. You just never know, do you?"

Patricia Pratico, whose teaching made an impact on student's lives.

"I couldn't leave teaching alone . . . but the focus changed to tutoring in the literacy program. I've had 69 students and the highest thrill was a 63-year-old Vietnamese woman who learned to read and write English so she could become an American citizen. I received the Jefferson Award for assisting in this program. Other awards have been sprinkled throughout but the people who become better, who learn to read and write are the ones who earned the awards."

Jen Southworth, who made a major difference in my life back those many years ago. L.S.

80 YOU REALIZE RETIREMENT ISN'T FOR EVERYONE

"I have no intention of retiring. Goodness! It would be terrible to have to get up every morning and play golf the way I play golf. Maybe something's going to come along that intrigues me more than newscasting. But so far I haven't found it."
Paul Harvey, from **Insight***, August 5, 1991.*

"As long as there's opportunity, I'm going to preach. No one in the Bible ever retired."
Billy Graham, evangelist for the world.

"Do what you want. When I say don't retire, that doesn't mean that seniors shouldn't change jobs. More than anything, it's important that senior citizens be in something they really like to do. . . stay active but stay active doing what *you* want to do."
Dave Thomas, from his book **Dave's Way.**

"Guess I'll never really retire. I love my work too much. I tell people, as long as you're physically able, I'll find something for you to do. I like what I'm doing now better than anything because I'm helping a lot of other people. I don't take anyone in unless they're at least 50 years old."

Bob Rheinhart, founder of Retiree Skills, Inc.

"It is wonderful to be at 70 and not have to retire. I'm sure if I worked for someone else, they'd retire me, but now I meet the general public, no two days are ever alike, and I have all these endless creative possibilities ahead. I can write, design new ceramic pieces, run my travel agency, my gift shop, and enjoy."

Jade Snow Wong, who has no time or desire to retire.

81 RETIREMENT MEANS ANYTHING YOU WANT IT TO MEAN

"I now wake up each morning looking forward to the day, no regrets. When I worked for a national company, I hated getting up in the morning. There's no longer any security there, the companies are running scared, forcing people out. Now I'm free."

Bob Allen, former employee.

"When you retire you're more experienced and wiser than ever before, you have no job restraints and fewer obligations, and you've never had more time at your disposal. It's a wonderful opportunity to try new activities like writing, speaking, and helping others restore identity, confidence and self-esteem through an organization of your choice. Mine is Toastmasters."

Thomas Montalbo, DTM.

"As the third phase of your life, (the first is your school days, the second your necessary occupation to earn a living) this is the period of true free-lancing, of uncommitted activity, the opportunity to engage in the occupation of your choice on your terms . . . you are the boss, the only boss."

*Harry Disston, in his book **Wear Out, Don't Rust Out**.*

"Walter always jokes that he wants to retire on a 60-foot boat with a 20-year-old mistress but he more likely will end up on his 48-foot boat with his 60-plus wife."

*Betsy Cronkite, sailing with her husband somewhere off the East Coast, from **Modern Maturity**.*

"Since I've retired I don't have the constant competition I faced when I worked. Satisfying the boss, the hassles of customers, tight schedules, all that took a toll on me, probably more than I realized at the time.

"Now I try to keep the jungle back out of our yard, you know like in those movies you see where it creeps back up on you. But I love yardwork. Our pontoon boat is tied up here in front of our house on the bay. We do a lot of crabbing, keep our Blue Gulf crabs alive in our basket on the pier until we're ready to steam them."

John McWhorter, who seems to be having a dreamed-of retirement on a bay right off the Gulf of Mexico.

YOU DEVELOP INCREASED INTEREST IN SOCIAL CHANGE AND POLITICS

"I've lived 70 years, my entire lifespan, stuck under the threat of communism, and now to see the changes that are happening are so exciting as to be almost unbelievable. There is such potential now for growth."

Louise Lothspeich, counselor.

"I'm strongly happy and grateful to have moved through the times of integration here in our country. While I know there is still much to be done for the Chinese or Asians to be fully accepted, when you look back, we have come a long way. Now I am glad for my background of being raised in a traditional Chinese home. I see ethnicity as a plus, not a minus."

Dr. Effie Chow, founder of The East/West Academy of Healing Arts.

Rosa Parks rocked the nation when she refused to give a white man her seat on the bus in Alabama. Her act of defiance led to the downfall of segregated busing. On her 79th birthday she told a crowd of 1,000 people, "I am still active and working diligently in every way I know how, to make our lives meaningful. I'm working toward the goal of freedom we are still seeking."

Rosa Parks, civil rights pioneer and heroine for the ages.

"I'm glad I've lived long enough to see a lessening in racial tensions."

John Hughes, from either the mid-west or the sunbelt, depending on the season.

"One of the good things for me has been all our country has done. I would never have dreamed that we would be landing men on the moon. Or that the Berlin Wall would come down. And to think that Russia has abandoned communism, who would have believed it. You know I was sort of young when the Wright Brothers flew their first plane and now we send the space shuttle up on a regular basis. We did all this in my lifetime, now if I could live long enough to hear they found life on another planet."

*Hazel Stout, adventurer, in the **Guiness Book of Records** as the oldest sky diver.*

"I've learned how important it is to exercise your body but exercising your mind is even more critical. In later life, people have more time to keep up with world happenings, what's going on in America and even right next door. When I think of all that has happened in my lifetime, I'm amazed and awed. And if I didn't keep my mind active, I'd miss out on so much."

Ruth Stafford Peale, who still writes, speaks, and helps run a massive ministry, The Peale Foundation.

"World peace is one of the best things about getting older. I've lived long enough to see the wall come down, the Russian empire dissolve and rulers in the Mid-East coming to the peace table."

*Dr. Norman Vincent Peale, pastor, preacher, author of many books, first being **The Power of Positive Thinking.***

"Because of my involvement with MIA's from Vietnam, I've learned that one of the greatest things about our political system is that one can work within the system and change it. One person can make a difference. I, and many others, firmly believe we have up to 2,000 prisoners left in Vietnam. Because of the efforts of those who care, the government is finally doing something about this situation again.

"I went to Vietnam believing my country right or wrong and couldn't understand the reactions of the anti-war demonstrators in the '60s and '70s. Now I realize that human beings run our government, men and women who are human and make mistakes. But that's the way life is. And it doesn't change the fact that, mistakes and all, this is still the greatest country in the world. The only one where people from other countries are still breaking down the doors to get in."

Retired Navy Capt. Eugene B. "Red" McDaniel, who lives by his convictions.

"I'm thinking of writing a major concern like J.C. Penney a letter saying 'I'm Robert C. Allen, your customer,' and giving them all the guidelines on how to treat their preferred customers. Businesses, government, everyone needs to remember how to treat their customers, the people who come to them. The notion of good service may be out of date but it's critical, especially now."

Bob Allen, a small business owner who wants this nation to return to a policy of good service.

YOU LEARN THAT SUCCESS CAN STILL COME AFTER 50

"God first, family second and business third. That's my recipe for success."
Mary Kay, founder of Mary Kay Cosmetics, Inc. after the age of 50.

"Things turn out best for the people who make the best of the way things turn out."
John Wooten, one of the winningest basketball coaches ever.

"People think I'm lucky. I just tell them, the harder I work, the luckier I get."
Bob Rheinhart, who founded the successful Retiree Skills corporation.

To create the Jewish widow who ages from 72 to 97 in *Driving Miss Daisy*, Jessica Tandy said, "I just have to let my memory take me back and my imagination take me forward. That's not hard when you have plenty of both in your 80s."
This movie, which earned her an Oscar, was her first major part in a movie. Miss Tandy is best known for her stage work.

[To be successful] "Don't fall in love with your bed."
Carol Channing, actress.

"To be successful in any kind of business, you need a hell of a lot of guts. That's the key word. Applies to growing older too."
Bob Rheinhart, who's made a success of Retiree Skills, Inc. in the last half of his life.

"How come [I'm successful]? . . . I'm in a hurry because I may not have much time." His advice for success: "Get off the g– d–- golf course."
Walter Lappert, a 68-year-old "retired" businessman whose new ice cream business grossed $30 million in one year, knows something about success.

"I think those of us who are older know that it takes a lot of hard work to be a success. You don't come to work on time and leave on time — you come early and leave late! Success is not an accident of good luck. I hate to say this, but it doesn't seem to be a major lesson taught to young people today."
A successful businesswoman.

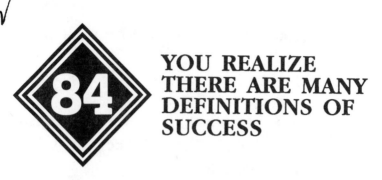

YOU REALIZE THERE ARE MANY DEFINITIONS OF SUCCESS

"One of my successes has been 30 years of writing a daily diary. I wish I had started 20 years earlier but pens then were so messy, ink splattered everywhere. I started when the ballpoint pen came into being. I got the idea when I came into possession of diaries from aunts and uncles. I've written over a million and a quarter words, granted there is some repetition, about my life as a farmer, my daily activities and my feelings through the years. I think I'll donate them to a University as an historical collection."

Leonard Tworek, farmer historian.

"Success isn't counted in a title but in the joys you get and give in life."

*First Lady Barbara Bush, from **Ladies Home Journal**, November 1990.*

"I read something once that I've used a lot. One, everybody should plant a tree. We've planted five Christmas trees in our back yard. Two, everybody should write a book. I'm up to 13 now. Three, everybody should have a child. We've had five.

We've always kind of overdone things.

"Now I'm into Population Zero which doesn't exactly fit with what we did. But if the three above are a measure of success, I'm doing okay."

Dr. Lendon H. Smith, sort-of-retired pediatrician.

"I never held a job outside my home and sometimes I wondered if maybe I was missing out on something. You know, I see these women all dressed up and in such a hurry all the time. And I think maybe I should go back to school or even go flip hamburgers at the local drive-in.

"But then, who would feed my birds or make a pie or hot dish for someone who's ailin'? Who would write letters to my children and my sisters? Who would take care of Momma when she needs help? I used to think these things weren't really important, but my daughter sat me down one day and really lit into me. Once she was done telling me all the important things I do, I felt pretty good. Maybe my flowers that show up on the church altar and at friends' houses are more than just pretty. Why, she even made me promise to keep all those letters I've been saving. Success wasn't a term I'd have used for me, but my daughter did."

A woman who has made a success out of life.

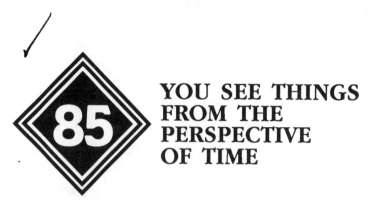

YOU SEE THINGS FROM THE PERSPECTIVE OF TIME

"When things happen in your life, at the moment they seem tremendously important. Like when the car won't start and you're late for an appointment. Or the roof leaks. Or you lose your job or you have a fight with a family member. Later when you look back, you may realize that what happened was insignificant — or perhaps tremendously important. I don't think young people, without the experience of time, can understand these things as easily as older people. Ask yourself, 'Will this be important in ten or twenty years?' "

Jean Collins, editor.

"When you look back on history, the importance of events and people frequently appears much different than it seemed at the time. The real impact of political decisions is much clearer years later — the place the current President of the United States may hold in history isn't known yet. One of the benefits of growing older is being able to see such things from the perspective of time."

P.B., looking at the big picture.

86 TIME BECOMES MORE PRECIOUS

"During the past five years time has grown more precious and I am less likely to waste it on projects or people I don't like. I have realized that I must take action in the pursuit of my dreams or risk having them remain unfulfilled."
Karen Blaker, Ph.D., in **Celebrating Fifty.**

"Now that my life is past the mid-point, there just isn't time to waste on the things that are unimportant to me. And I don't feel guilty. I used to. Be polite, all that. Not anymore. There just isn't enough time to do all I want."
Phil Oestricher.

"The main difference in my interests now and when I was younger, is that now I have the time to spend on them. My time is even more precious now because it is mine."
Erma Giddings, who is enjoying her new life.

"All my life I worked hard as a nurse and farmer and wife and mother, there was never time for church or the other volunteer things I wanted to do. My three children were active in 4-H so we all did the fairs and dairy shows, while at the same time keeping the home farm of dairy and chickens running.

"Now that I'm retired time is still precious and I never have enough of it. I love working at the church; circle and quilting, Bible studies and Altar Guild. It's like I'm making up for all those years when I only got to attend Sunday services on my weekends off. I've made so many friends through my activities that even though I've buried two husbands, I know I'm loved and valued. And I have plenty of people to love and care for."

Thelma Sommerseth, 79 and making up for lost time.

87 YOU HAVE TIME FOR THINKING, FOR REFLECTION

"All my life, if I was going to do any thinking, I had to stay awake all night to do it. Now I have the time for deep thinking in the daytime so I can sleep at night."

Hazel Rue, who uses her thinking time to make life better for those around her.

"Now that I am no longer teaching and being an administrator at the Linus Carl Pauling Institute of Science and Medicine, I have more time for research and to think about things. I concentrate on research, thinking about and trying to solve scientific problems. It's a good thing I'm a theoretical researcher rather than a laboratory researcher. I don't think I could physically handle working so many hours in a laboratory but my mind never quits."

Dr. Linus Carl Pauling, winner of two Nobel prizes, 90 years old and still going strong.

"When you reach a certain age, it's like you're on this hill and you can see so much better. You can see where you've been and you can see where you're going. Maybe you don't have so far to go so it's easier to look ahead. I've become much more reflective, almost a spiritual experience."

Jim Bosley, TV weatherman and talk show host.

"I definitely think we become more reflective as we get older. I know I try to see the end result, rather than just doing it at the time. What will the result be? Only once in awhile do I look back and think how I might have improved a situation had I done something differently. I long since have accepted it as it is. [As I got older] I found myself looking ahead more."

Hazel Van Marter, at 90 still reflecting on the future.

"I used to only be able to think when I took a bath, but now that the children are grown, I can take time for myself, for thinking."

P.D., mother of six and grandmother of 13.

88 YOU HAVE TIME FOR HOBBIES

"I love to cook. All the years I worked, I never had the time. Now I love it. My wife says I make all these wonderful meals, fancy things so now I do most of our cooking. I even clean up after myself, gives me a good feeling."

Dick Cavnar, 67 and cooking up a storm.

"I finally have time for crafts. I love pottery, I work with a wheel myself and love to share that skill with others. Now that I'm no longer chasing children or helping run an apple ranch, I can focus on shapes and colors, on the wonder of a new pot forming within my hands. I'm teaching a class too, here at the retirement home where I moved. Next to creating my own things, I get a thrill out of helping others learn and seeing their joy when they hold their new creation for the first time."

Helen Bryant, potter at a retirement village.

"I have freedom in trying out new recipes on the other people at our senior citizen's group. Otherwise we would be eating such large recipes for a month."

Mazie Maxey, artist.

"These days I work out in a gym twice a week, play recorders and gambas (a type of stringed instrument), go to poetry class once a week, attend lots of concerts and love my old age. I thank God daily for His great kindness to me."
David Goldstein, M.D., poet and composer.

"We've taken up golf, now about four or five couples go up to Carolina for a week to play. We just never had time to do that when we were younger."
Bob and Dale Allen.

"I love writing so one of my hobbies now is to send cards and letters to those who are ill in our church, or who need encouragement. I stick in cartoons, stickers, whatever might help make their day brighter. I've been collecting sayings from all kinds of sources for years so usually I'll start a letter with a famous or not-so famous quote. I especially love working with kids who have cancer or some such life-threatening illness. One 12-year-old and I have become fast friends because we both write poetry. Now we swap verses. I didn't have time for something like this when I was younger."
Elaine Aspelund, poet, encourager and friend.

"When I'm not taking care of the rental units my daughter and I own, I love playing in the sand pile. You know, planting flowers, gardening. One thing I've decided about the fall, fallen leaves are beautiful, brown is pretty. Otherwise the raking and trimming gets to be too much so I learn to adapt, to make it work for me."

Kathleen Fuller, wise gardener.

"One day I told my daughter that I'd like to write about our family and wouldn't you know, I opened the paper sent out by the school district and there it said, 'Write Your Life's Story.' It took me two and a half years off and on but I finished it. I am so pleased I did it. My entire family, even to the nieces and nephews, are delighted I did this. I just wish I'd started earlier and recorded my grandmother's wonderful stories. I've started my husband's story now."

Dollie Root, family historian.

"Everywhere we went in our years in the military, I would learn the history of the area. When we moved to Bremerton, I found a treasure. Bremerton Naval Shipyard and the town of Bremerton were founded in 1891. As I dug out facts and interviewed people, I ran across pictures and soon was presenting slide shows about the history. This all culminated in a book I helped create for the centennial celebration. It's called *NIPSIC to Nimitz, A Centennial History of the Puget Sound Naval Shipyard,* and is in its second printing. It's a great book, 300 pages, hard cover, beautiful pictures, more of a coffee table edition. Had no idea how much I'd learn

when I started playing around with the history of this area. My hobby became a real job."
Louise M. Reh, volunteer historian.

"I've become a collector as I grow older, of things that please me, not because they have monetary value. We do Christmas in a major way with three theme trees up in the house. Then I display my collection of Santas and Dicken's village. I love tea pots, pewter, both tiny and antique. Teddy bears take up a corner in the bedroom. It seems that by the time I have two of anything, it quickly becomes a collection."
Sally Stuart, who must like dusting.

"I found that I needed another hobby for when I retire, so I read all the books and magazines I could on the stock market. I wanted to understand the flow of the numbers and how the business worked. Then I realized that to really understand it, you had to take a risk with some of your own money. I did all right, but when work got too overwhelming, I put the market on hold 'til retirement. Then I'll be able to give it the focus and time needed. I stay pretty relaxed about my investment choices. I have the theory that there are hundreds of trains leaving the station. If I didn't make that one, there's another one coming."
Phil Oestricher, 60, turning in his planes for the stock market.

ELDERHOSTEL IS A FANTASTIC WAY TO TRAVEL AND LEARN

Elderhostel is an educational program for older adults who want to continue to expand their horizons and to develop new interests and enthusiasms. It's for elder citizens on the move, not just in terms of travel, but in terms of intellectual activity as well. Its commitment is to the belief that retirement does not represent an end to significant activity for older adults but a new beginning filled with opportunities and challenges.

With Elderhostel, participants enjoy inexpensive, short-term academic programs at educational institutions around the world. Elderhostel students live on the campus of their host institution while attending a program and have access to the cultural and recreational facilities and resources available there. For more information, write to:

Elderhostel
80 Boylston Street, Suite 400
Boston, MA 02116

"My wife and I have enjoyed eight domestic Elderhostel programs and two foreign ones over the past three years. The mental stimulation of the Elderhostel programs makes it more rewarding than any other type of travel."

Leonard and Margery Staugas will do it again!

"My first, and so far only, experience of Elderhostel took place at Holden Village, a conference grounds that used to be a mining camp high in the Cascade mountains above Lake Chelan. That place has to be one of the most beautiful in the world. The accommodations were comfortable and the food good. A professor from Washington State University taught one class on animals called 'All About Pigs: Showing Animal Value to Humans.' The man who years before had been in charge of the mine there taught geology and an artist tried to convince us all that we could draw.

"Being back in class was a bit of a shock, it's too many years since I was a student, but I'd go again — give me half an hour to pack."

T.C.S., a happy camper.

"Elderhostel welcomes anyone 60 or older to attend one-week courses in colleges and other institutions of learning across the country and around the world. For $250 per week including room and board, you or I can study Greek Mythology at Mississippi State, Architecture of Cape Breton in Nova

Scotia . . . languages, cooking, computers, archeology, religion and crafts are included in the myriad of offerings for the same fee. And each $205 entitles the student to three courses, not just one. Of course the dormitories are not like the Ritz, and cafeteria food is not like dining at the River Cafe, but the groups are like-minded people of our own age, which sounds like congeniality plus to me."

*Frances Weaver, in her book, **The Girls With the Grandmother Faces**. Frances has attended a variety of sessions, as have many of her friends. She believes it's a good way to see the world and keep the mind sharp at the same time.*

I CAN'T

90 YOU HAVE TIME TO TRAVEL

"We're in McCall, Idaho where husband Phil can ski and I can read and write. That's one of the great things about adding years to the lifetime tally. You can finally afford a vacation that is not a camping trip or to visit relatives."
Aris Painter, nurse executive.

"You not only get to take vacations when you want but you can travel in the middle of the week. There's less traffic, fewer crowds and less tension all around."
A relaxed traveler.

"I had a friend tell me, 'Grace, do your traveling before your feet hurt too much and your girdle gets too tight.' I believed her and after my husband died from a five-year bout with cancer, traveling to Europe with an old friend of mine who spoke marvelous French, was wonderful medicine."
Grace Parker, who still likes to travel.

"I had an opportunity to travel but for a person with a panic disorder, the thought was overwhelming. But I said to myself, 'What's the worst thing that can happen?' If I have a panic attack and there's no one to help me and I drop dead — so what. That's okay too. But I found that when I got panicky, I just coped. So I've traveled Europe, parts of the Mediterranean, Northern Africa and Morroco. There we were driving in the desert, couldn't speak the language, couldn't read the signs but I coped. I found out that my 'stricken' look works well, gets people to help me in spite of language."

Pat Smith, who has adventures in spite of her panic attacks.

"Guess you could call us Snowbirds. In fact, we've worn out one trailer and have put plenty of miles on the second one. We've driven our rig from coast to coast with lots of trips to our son's house in Minnesota. There's relatives in Florida, Texas, Colorado, Minnesota and California that we like to visit. We have a membership in Naco, a campground organization, and we've sure met a lot of new people and made great friends traveling from campground to campground. We head south just after Christmas and return to the Pacific Northwest after the snow leaves the passes. We hit the Midwest in the spring or early fall. We always wanted to travel, and we'll keep doing this as long as we're able. Winter in Arizona or Southern California sure beats the rain and cold of home."

The Glandons, confirmed snowbirds.

YOU CAN SHARE YOUR KNOWLEDGE AND EXPERIENCE

"I love receiving calls for advice from younger nurse managers just plotting their careers; helping them avoid the pitfalls and showing them where to concentrate their education dollars for the most benefit."

Aris Painter, nurse executive.

"When people ask my advice, I tell them, 'The world is crying out for people who can make decisions. A good leader learns to delegate. Spend your time on the thing that is most profitable and hire someone else to do the more menial tasks.' "

Marlys Gilbert, who is a font of wisdom, all learned and filtered through years of experience.

"My advice: Find the good and praise it."
*Alex Hailey, author of **Roots**, on **The Meaning Of Life** on CBS*

"[My advice is] 'Praise people to success . . . now our company motto . . . the only way to do business.' "
Mary Kay Ashe, founder of Mary Kay products.

"My advice to seniors is, 'Take a walk on the wild side'. . . all the fun seniors I have ever met were a little eccentric. Wait 'til my kids see what I have planned for myself . . ."

*R. David Thomas, founder of Wendy's restaurant franchises, in **Dave's Way**.*

"Best advice . . . make sure you have something to do — have a reason to get up in the morning."

*Lucille Ball, actress, from **Old Age Is Not For Sissies** by Art Linkletter.*

"It's our place to educate younger people, in a nice way but firmly. Like when you're in a store and two younger people are gabbing rather than waiting on you. I read somewhere that an older, very successful woman was standing in line to be waited on. The clerk was rude and rushed. The woman leaned closer and said nicely but firmly, 'Dear, I have something important to tell you. I'm profit, you're overhead.' I wish I'd said that."

Birdie Etchison, starting a new life again.

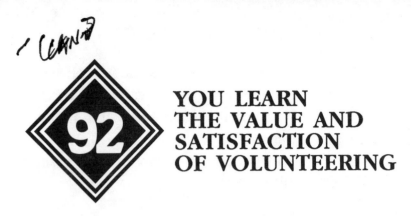

I LEARNED

YOU LEARN THE VALUE AND SATISFACTION OF VOLUNTEERING

Betty West, a widow, lived in Pennsylvania when her daughter volunteered for the Peace Corps as a nurse.

"When I visited her in Central Africa, I was so proud of her. So a few months later, I quit my job as a paralegal and spent two years teaching English in Thailand. Some mornings I woke up thinking, 'What am I doing here?' But it was rewarding. I had the satisfaction of helping others improve their lives. I liked the Asian theory on age. They thought I was very important just because I had lived all those years. Thanks to my daughter, I now work for the Peace Corps as a recruiter."

Betty West now assists other "seniors"— Peace Corps terminology for volunteers over 50.

About your heart:

If individuals are ambitious, competitive, or under pressure for purely selfish reasons, they may be at greater risk than if they are ambitious or competitive to serve others or higher ideals. Ironically, the best way to save one's own heart may be loving and caring for others.

Irwin Bottemiller never married and had children of his own, so after retiring from chicken farming, he moved into town and found lots of kids to call him "Grandpa Irwin." All his kids "need a lot of love and affection" because they and their parents are homeless or in retraining programs.

"I work with the little ones at two different programs and then at Sunday School. It's pure fun. Almost like a full-time job, but I need to keep busy. When those little ones run up and throw their arms around my knees — well, there's just nothing like it."

"Grandpa Irwin" Bottemiller, retired farmer.

"I think building houses for poor families is a much clearer demonstration of those qualities [of concern for people] than trying to serve in the political world. But I don't feel that I've changed at all. It's just a matter of changing times, changing opinions and changing priorities."

*Jimmy Carter on Habitat for Humanity, in **Good Housekeeping**, January 1992.*

Those who do volunteer work report significantly higher degrees of good health than those who do not.
*From **Society**, March/April 1981*

"I'm 85 and I've lived here most of my life so

taking part in the community is a big part of my life. I've been on all kinds of committees and boards but the most recent one is [that I am] chairman of the Davies Library Board. I thought, Dot, what are you doing? But then life has always been a challenge and I like it that way. I'm kind of like that children's story about the little engine that said 'I think I can. I think I can.' Well, the term's for three years and 'I think I can.' "

Dot Latting, plantation owner.

"Since I've moved to my new house on a lake, I've gotten involved in the community very quickly. I take some classes, write, serve on a local board with ecological concerns and now something that uses my professional background. I help seniors with their income tax through AARP. It's the kind of one on one, personal serving that I like best."

Erma Giddings, 65, from a small town with friendly people.

"A good thing about retirement is that now you have time for a third or fourth career, maybe without pay. I was a teacher all my life but really thought sometimes of switching over to law enforcement. When I retired, I volunteered to teach the three R's at the county jail with a population of 400. Took me three years to get in there, they'd look at me and say, 'What does that little old lady know about these naughty boys,' but I finally made it.

"I'd taught kids with learning and emotional problems in school and this was no different. About half the inmates are dyslexic, can't tell left from right, can't cross the medial line. I believe this is the main reason for criminality. Learning to read made major differences in their lives."
Hazel May Rue, who made a difference.

"If we can get people to read we can get them out of the jails and the shelters and off the streets and back to work. I believe this is the most important issue we have and that's why I'm glad to give support to the cause."
*First Lady Barbara Bush on her primary volunteer effort, from **People Magazine**, November, 1988.*

"I speak to school children because I feel it is important to give back. I tell them, many of whom are minorities, everyone is talented, but you have to look for your talent and work to develop it. All of you must learn English well to get ahead in your field, not matter what you choose. You have to be able to express yourself. And you must give something back to society. America with all its ills and problems has given a lot to minorities."
Jade Snow Wong, who teaches by example.

"Besides taking care of yourself and learning what you need to be healthy, giving something to others is the best medicine around. So I volunteer at a school that helps girls from off the street. We get them well. I help with a local theater group and at a naturopathic college. I'm a bit of a turncoat since I believe in chiropractic and naturopathic medicine. But people need to be in charge of their own health. And need to be serving others."

Dr. Lendon H. Smith, a boat rocker by choice.

"I'm really fortunate because since I left the school system where I taught, I've never had to work to earn a living. But I like making money and seem to have a real talent for it. So when an organization needs funding, I jump right in.

"I've helped libraries, reading programs and even got a grand piano for the community. It has a lot to do with the people you know, but you must be willing to ask, ask, ask."

Grace Parker, who loves a benefit.

"I found that if you were hungry and had no money, there was no place to get a hot meal. To me, food is one of your basic needs, so I took on the challenge of the Daily Bread Soup Kitchen. We garner enough donations from restaurants and charitable agencies so none of our budget is spent on food. There've been problems with City Hall, neighbors, a day that includes enough pressures for three days. I thrive on challenges. We have fun here. I tell my 200 to 400 volunteers, 'You're not getting paid, so if you don't have fun here, you're missing the boat.'

"One of my great rewards is that we've been able to fight for human dignity. The more we can bring on ounce of loving kindness to our guests' lives, the more they'll believe in love again and go back to fight for their own lives."

Diane Hayward, who lives to serve others. From **New Choices***, Dec. 1991/Jan. 1992.*

"I love the parks around here, they were established in the 1860's, and have been allowed to deteriorate. So I volunteer for the Knights in Armor who've come to the aid of the parks. I'd done a slide show on one of the parks and we used that for publicity. I've pleaded before the city council, picketed in front of the television camera, things I never dreamed I'd do.

"I also volunteer at a science museum. I thought that since I'm a scientist, I'd get to work with the collection, but unfortunately they found out I had talents in campaigning for funds which I certainly didn't want to do. I hate the telephone and they give me all these cards of people to call and I get money out of them. I don't know how I do it. But there I am."

Ruth Heintz, whose volunteer work has taken over her photography interests.

"I believe that we need to educate our country's

children about patriotism, about the values of our nation. Everyone needs to learn pride in themselves and pride in their country. So with Pride of America, we have speakers go into the schools and talk with the kids and pump them up about what a great country we live in."

*Retired Capt. Red McDaniel, author of **Scars and Stripes** and founder of Pride of America.*

93 YOU HAVE MANY INTERESTING HOUSING OPTIONS

"I didn't do a lot of looking around for a retirement home because I had friends who lived in this one. Right away I felt at home. It's comforting to know that other people with my same interests are right around me. I entertain a lot because I love having people around and everyone is near so we don't have to worry about driving in the dark and such. We travel together, just got back from three weeks in Hawaii. I take part in all kinds of activities and just have fun, making up for all the things I didn't have time for before."

Helen Bryant, enjoying life in a life-care facility overlooking a scenic valley.

"After my husband died, I sold our home and moved into the city. The suburbs are no place for an attractive widow, so family-oriented and with nothing to do in the evenings. The city of San Francisco offers opera, theater, symphony, so you can go out every night if you like. I bought a house in Presidio Heights, a beautiful section, and not long after an old friend moved in with me. His wife had died several years before. He thought we should get married but I didn't want to be tied down again after going through the years of cancer with my husband (although we married later). So we just had a wonderful time, picnics at the Arboretum in Golden Gate Park, entertaining, serving on boards. It was a dream life, the kind you read about in romances.

"Until cancer struck me. When I was on the road to recovery again, we decided the house was too much and looked for a retirement community. But we had a slight problem. My new husband, Hubbell Parker, had passed the age requirement. He was now in his 90s, but you'd never know it to look at him. Now five years later he stills swims every day, takes me dancing and even traveling, though now we stay closer to home.

"Our move to Spring Lake was just what we needed. I found out the library system up here was in trouble so I had a new project. Our neighbors are great and the services here at the retirement community fit the bill. It's just another chapter in our storybook romance."

Grace Parker, who is always looking for solutions to new challenges.

"Several of us widows got together and bought a house so we wouldn't be so lonely. Then we decided that having a younger man around to help with maintenance would be a good idea so we advertised an apartment available with specifics. Now we share the cooking and household chores. Our renter bought into our little community, and in return for meals takes care of the lawn, the heavy stuff and our cars. We're all happy with the arrangement. It's a creative way to solve housing problems for older people."

Hazel White and her cohorts, who were willing to try something new.

"I have a big, old house that has been in our family for three generations. My husband and I remodeled it by adding several bathrooms, insulation, that kind of thing. When he died, my children lived too far away to want the house and I really didn't want to leave it. But I felt like a marble rattling around in a huge box.

"One day down at the senior center, I mentioned that I was thinking about opening it up to a boarder or two. Within a week, I had four requests. Two older gentlemen and two ladies. All of them moved in and now we're a family. At first I did the cooking and cleaning the main part of the house, but now we all pitch in. That way everyone feels useful and I think we're all younger for it.

"At first my son had a fit, but now he just laughs. My daughter brings her children to visit and the grandchildren have a whole bunch of grandmas and grandpas. It's working for us and so far we're all healthy. I think the gardening we all do helps also."

Genny Marsh, who filled her need and others' as well.

94

YOU LEARN NOT TO FEAR DYING

"In China the elderly are treated with respect. Because aging is part of living, we learn to grow old with grace and wisdom. Why fight it? Instead, use the wisdom you've learned and grow old gracefully. And then to die gracefully and with peace, that is the way life is meant to be because death is not a fearsome thing. Here is another area where my Chinese background and Western knowledge can combine to bring the best help to those around me."

Dr. Effie Chow, founder of The East/West Academy of Healing Arts.

"While I'm reasonably healthy and grateful for that, I don't fear the inevitable, in fact, I'm kind of curious about it. I plan to use the time 'til then enjoying life in whatever form it takes. I've realized I'm not immortal since a solid bout with cancer really opened my eyes. Made me more conscious of the value of time. There is not an infinite amount of time left, so I ought to do smart things with it. The key word is enjoy."

Phil Oestricher, pilot.

"Something else caring for my mother taught me was to get my own affairs in order. I absolutely refuse to make my children do the same for me. I've told my wife Karen and written out all my instructions so everyone knows exactly what to do, what I want.

"Due to a terrible storm when we were flying, we thought sure we were on our way out, my wife and I shared with each other the deep things you only talk about before death. I know how she feels about me and how I feel about her and who I am and what I've accomplished.

"Recently on vacation, when I lay in the surf cut up and bleeding due to a fall down the cliff, the thought of dying brought peace. I was okay."
Jim Bosley, talkshow host.

"It's up to you to die young, as late as possible."
Art Linkletter, who believes in the fountain of aging.

"There have been studies done that show we have a soul. A person was weighed just before death and just after. Four ounces had disappeared. So don't tell me there is no soul that leaves the body.

"Just like birth was a passage from one kind of life to another, so is death. It is not an end, it is a passage to another level of being, the highest level of being."
Elaine Aspelund, who as a nurse has held many hands on that passage.

YOU CAN GROW THROUGH THE LOSS OF YOUR SPOUSE

"I will always have a pocket of grief in my heart. How could it be otherwise? But that will not keep me from enjoying life. On the contrary, it will make me value every minute, because now I know how precious each one is."
*Dr. Joyce Brothers, from her book **Widowed**.*

"My husband died three years ago after a long battle with Parkinsons [disease]. After that I decided that I needed to enjoy life. My years are numbered too. As you get older you realize how lucky you are to live this number of years."
Velma Willarson, bird lover.

"I've been a widow for 31 years and while I don't talk about it a lot, I guess I teach by example. I've learned that it's up to me to make things happen. Like when I entertain. I always invite two couples and another widow. That way there are men around and we get their viewpoint too. I think too many widows wait for invitations and don't reach out to make their own lives richer."
Charlotte Murphy, a busy widow.

"When I lost my husband, we'd been married over 50 years, it was the most terrible thing that could have happened, worse than when my mother or father died. I didn't know how I was going to keep going. But I think I'd inherited perseverance from my mother. Her life was so hard but she set an example that I tried to live up to. That's what got me through.

"I'm still independent, living in the home I've owned since '39, and now I'm 92. I still go upstairs to my bedroom, the laundry is in the basement, and people love my kitchen like they always have."

Flora Euller, setting a good example.

"My husband died seven years ago and it was traumatic for me. We were so close. We ran our business together, then went home together at night. I feel that in the last year, I have finally adjusted to his death. Now I can travel without looking for him right beside me. While I think of him all the time, I do it with less pain.

"After he died, I refused to accept a lower standard of living. I worked very hard, we had our house, but hard work isn't bad. It kept me from being lonely. I bought a building, a car. There was a lot of homework there since I had to learn all about car ratings, purchasing property, my husband had done all those things. Each time I'd think, 'Well, I got through that one okay.' I continue to do the things I enjoyed before he died; entertain, take my children out to dinner, travel, run our businesses, write, create new colors when I fire my ceramics. I miss him, but I know I can get through."

Jade Snow Wong, continuing to live creatively.

"When I found myself suddenly alone . . . I felt a need to strengthen the connections to friends and family that I already had . . . . I made myself happy because I wanted to be happy. I consciously set out to learn what gave me pleasure, and I filled my life with those things. I taught myself what is really important — human relationships, giving of oneself to others, and making oneself generally useful in society — and devoted my life to the pursuit of the things tht would enhance those aspects of my existence.

"And I have made a good life for myself . . . I am extremely proud of what I have been able to accomplish."

*Philomene Gates, widow, attorney, author, in her book **Suddenly Alone**.*

"As you age you gain a strength that you can only get through endurance, through age."

Pat Smith, editor at a university press.

96 YOU BECOME MORE UNIQUE

"As you grow older, you are more and more unique. There is no else with your particular set of life experiences, insights and beliefs. These are your strengths, and they make you interesting to others. Cultivate this individuality. As you actively grow and change, your personal uniqueness increases. Your individuality is not set early in life, but develops as you age. Avoid conformity . . . don't let yourself become perfectly predictable."

James F. Fries, M.D., in Aging Well.

"What a marvelously simple truth! Gerontologists have observed for years that as persons age they seem to be less alike; each person expresses his or her own unique gifts. Lifestyles become more diverse — some take off the join the Peace Corps, others continue working and some sit in a big chair watching television. Few need to conform to peer pressures, so they do what they like."

Ann and Robert Redd, in Whimsey, Wit and Wisdom.

"I've become more of everything because I've gotten old."
Mary Ferreira, who's especially full of love and joy.

"I think the reason we each become more unique as we grow older is because we are a composite of all our heritage and our life experiences. No one else has the same experiences as I do, therefore no one else can be just like me.
Kathleen Harries, who rejoices in the uniqueness of every person she meets.

"It takes lots of years of living and experiences to gather enough courage to become the unique individual you were meant to be."
Rose Mason.

YOU NEVER OUTGROW YOUR NEED FOR HUGS

"As you grow older, you need to put your arms around each other more."
*Barbara Bush, in **Ladies Home Journal**, March 1990.*

> "Hugs and touch are desperately important as you grow older. We know from all the research on touch that it is extremely health-giving. When we are touched, we relax and to the degree we relax our muscles and diaphragm, relax and massage our organs. Therefore, we are healthier and have a stronger immune system. The ramifications of touch are awesome and we don't get enough. Particularly older people need more because they have less opportunity after their families move away."
> *C. Jay Hawkins, who brings healing through touch and hugs.*

"Hugs and kisses are so important, especially with your family members. I know my feelings on this come from my Hawaiian background. In the islands, everyone hugs and kisses everyone hello and goodbye. Besides that, I'm Portugese and we're a very emotional people. When I met my husband, he's from the cold Midwest and you know, they don't say or show anything. But, you know, now he and all his family hug. I think we talked them into it."

Jackie George, a dyed-in-the-wool hugger.

"A speaker I really like, Dr. Mark Victor Hansen, once said you need four hugs a day to be psychologically normal, eight for maintenance and twelve to grow. They learned this at the Self-Esteem Institute in Ohio. I think that many hugs is fantastic, so make sure you get your quota every day. Remember, Hug Day is even on the calendar now, but we need hugs every day."

Lauraine Snelling.

YOU LEARN TO ACCEPT WHAT YOU CANNOT CHANGE

"By the time you get older, you realize you just do the best you can. If a dear one dies, there's a divorce, an illness, you know that life isn't fair. But you can't let them change your whole life and make you a lesser person. Bitter disappointments in life either are going to make you a better person inside or less. You are not going to stay the same. Your attitude is the main thing you can do something about."
Art Linkletter.

"The basic secret of successful living, widowed or not, is serenity to accept the things we cannot change. One of the women I have admired for years make the remark after the death of her 80-year-old husband: 'Well, I guess I'll just have to accept the fact that he isn't here anymore.' What *else* was she going to do? Where are the choices?

"The rest of the Serenity Prayer applies particularly well to the shock of finding oneself adrift and alone after losing a spouse. Courage to change the things I can . . . and the wisdom to know the difference."
*Frances Weaver, in **The Girls With the Grandmother Faces.***

YOU LEARN TO ACCEPT AGING

> A national sampling of Americans over 60 classifies them this way: "enjoyers" (27 percent), "survivors" (53 percent), and "casualties" (20 percent).
> **Society**, *March/April 1981.*

"It isn't the growing old that bothers me, but being perceived as 'old.' "
*Kenny Rogers, singer, from **The Meaning of Life** on CBS.*

"You can't help getting older but you don't have to get old."
*George Burns, actor, from **The Meaning of Life** on CBS.*

"Age is a relative matter. If you continue to work and absorb the beauty of the world around you, you find that age doesn't necessarily mean getting old."
Pablo Casals, who was still playing concerts on his cello at 96.

> Baby boomers born between 1946 and 1965 make up nearly one-third of America's 248.7 million people.
> *Associated Press analysis of census data.*

"People are living longer these days. Plenty of people spend 20 to 25 years being a 'senior citizen.' The way I look at it, why not figure out how to do it right, right off the bat, when there are just 60 candles on the cake."

R. David Thomas, the Wendy's man, from his book **Dave's Way.**

"Age . . . is one of those invisible barriers that *other* people see you go through — but *you* never go through it. If you're a vital person, inside your head that same person is still going on."

Betty White, from **Old Age Is Not For Sissies** *by Art Linkletter.*

"I admit I used to worry that when you reached a certain age, things stopped happening. But I don't worry about that anymore because — and it's a pleasure to tell you — they don't stop happening. I haven't stopped doing anything because of my age."

Cary Grant in **Redbook,** *1987.*

"The years between 65 and 75 have been the best years of my life; best for work, best for making money, best for making love although less is more in that category."

*David Brown, from **The Rest of Your Life is the Best of Your Life.***

"I have to tell you that being old isn't such a handicap. In some ways it's a help. You can't do as much, and there may be things you can't do as well, but nobody expects you to. Old-timers don't have to come in first. They get credit for just showing up. And if they're out there making a real effort, they've got everyone pulling for them."

*George Burns, who insists he'll keep showing up after 100. From his book **Wisdom of the Nineties.***

"When I was 22, I said to myself, 'Mary, someday it's going to be important to be younger than you really are.' So from that moment on, I just kept lying about my age. Then last year, when I was about to turn 50, I couldn't contain myself anymore. I thought it was so fantastic to turn 50 and look as good as I looked, that I was practically stopping strangers on the street to tell them how old I really was."

*Mary Tyler Moore, in **Redbook**, May 1988.*

"Growing older isn't such a problem if you've done your homework when you were younger, putting in what was required to make life worthwhile now. I gave my four children the time they needed so now they are people I am proud of and close to. I put my career on hold for those years then had to pay attention every working day so now it's on a good cash basis. No worries about paying the bills.

"I did my exercises and watched my diet and now at 70, my body's not deteriorating like those I see around me. I like my life and I'm pleased with what I've accomplished. Doing my homework was worth it."

Jade Snow Wong, business owner.

"People *expect* you to be tired!"
A humorous woman who takes advantage of her age.

"I've made a conscious effort to avoid the trap most people fall into after they reach 60. All of a sudden they think they have to start looking and acting a certain way. They think they have to slow down, so they do . . . But I still do one-night stands and I always want to know where my next gig is. My whole life revolves around doing things better than before. There's always room for improvement."
*Bob Hope, from **The Saturday Evening Post**.*

"Years wrinkle the skin, but to give up enthusiasm wrinkles the soul."
Samuel Ullman.

GROWING OLDER

Who is this person I see when I look in the
    glass?
I know it is I, though not the I I know.
The skin, the hair, the freshness, where did they
    go?
That I is almost vanished, let it pass.
It seems at times that my life is all in the past.
Not long ago, the span between two springs
Seemed huge and full of unexpected things.
Now the years run together, each like the last.
Shall I repine for what the years destroy?
So much is lost! Well, say that is true,
So much remains — I live, have things to do.
People to love, beauty to enjoy.
Aware of what's lost, I learn what I have, and
    say —
I will never again be as young as I am today.
David Goldstein, 1986.

"How do I stay vigorous at my advanced age of 74?
Apparently I have the right genes. More seriously,
my secret is having things to do — being interested
and involved in life and wanting to do lots more
than I have already done."
*Walter Cronkite, from **Modern Maturity**.*

"God saves the best wine for last."
Kristen Johnson Ingram, writer, philosopher.

"You are as young as your faith, as old as your
doubt, as young as your hope, as old as your
despair. So long as your heart receives messages of
beauty, cheer, courage, grandeur and power from

the earth, from man and from the Infinite, so long you are young.

"When the wires are all down and the central place of your heart is covered with the snows of pessimism and the ice of cynicism, then you are grown old indeed and may God have mercy on your soul."

*Samuel Ullman, from **I Dare You! How to Stay Young Forever.***

THE FUTURE HOLDS
ONLY ANTICIPATION

"I've been asked to write my memoirs. Hell, no — I'm still living my memoirs. I can't stop to spend time in the past when I'm living each day to the fullest. To me, every new day is as important as yesterday."

*Elizabeth Taylor, from **Good Housekeeping**, February 1992.*

"I've never had any particular feeling about my age. I've never felt like I ever missed anything; I never experienced a middle-age crisis and I've never regretted the beginning of a new decade. Age has never had an impact on anything I enjoy. For me, the future holds only anticipation."

Art Linkletter.

BIBLIOGRAPHY

Age Wave, Ken Dychtwald, Ph.D., Los Angeles:
Jeremy Tarcher 1989

Aging Well, James F. Fries, M.D., Reading, MA:
Addison-Wesley 1989

As Far As I Can See, Frances Weaver, Los Angeles:
Price Stern Sloan 1991

Celebrating 50, Karen Blaker, Ph.D., Chicago:
Contemporary Books 1990

I Dare You, Lucile Bogue, San Leandro, CA:
Bristol Publishing Enterprises 1990

It's Better To Be Over the Hill Than Under It, Eda
LeShan, New York: New Market Press 1990

Life Begins at 50, Leonard Hansen, New York:
Barron's 1989

Lifetrends, Jerry Gerber, et. al., New York:
McMillan Publishing 1989

Living Well, Teresa Herring, North Hollywood, CA:
Newcastle Publishing 1991

Me, Katherine Hepburn, New York: Random
House, Inc. 1991

Midlife Musings, Frances Weaver, Los Angeles:
Price Stern Sloan 1991

Old Age is Not for Sissies, Art Linkletter, New York:
Viking Penguin 1988

Retirement, Leo Hauser and Vincent A. Miller,
Wayzata, MN: DCI Publishing, Inc. 1989

Sex Over 40, Saul Rosenthal, Los Angeles: Jeremy
Tarcher 1987

Start Your Own Business After 50, Lauraine Snelling, San Leandro, CA: Bristol Publishing Enterprises, Inc. 1990

Suddenly Alone, Philomene Gates, New York: Harper Perennial 1990

The Creative Journal, Lucia Capacchione, Ph.D., North Hollywood, CA: Newcastle Publishing, Inc. 1989

The Girls With The Grandmother Faces, Frances Weaver, Los Angeles: Price Stern Sloan 1987

To Love Again, Florence Mason, San Francisco: Gateway Books 1989

Wear Out, Don't Rust Out, Harry Disston, White Hall, VA: Better Way Publications, Inc. 1989

Whimsey, Wit and Wisdom, Ann and Robert Redd, Ada, MI: Thornapple Publishing Co. 1990

Widowed, Dr. Joyce Brothers, New York: Simon and Schuster 1990

Wisdom of the Nineties, George Burns, New York: G.P. Putnam and Sons 1991

Women Coming of Age, Jane Fonda, New York: Simon and Schuster 1984